RHYTHMS OF THE WORLD

EDITED BY
FRANCIS HANLY AND TIM MAY

BBC BOOKS

Picture Credits

Front cover picture © BBC (photo Robert Hill).
Page 4 Mary Evans Picture Library

Paris Africa: page 11 Iain McKell; pages 12 and 14 (top) Jak Kilby; page 14 (below) BBC (photo Robert Hill); pages 14–15, 16 and 17 Collection Viollet; pages 19 and 20 (top) Jak Kilby; page 20 (below) BBC (photo Robert Hill); pages 20–21 Patrick Aventurier/Gamma/Spooner; page 21 Adrian Boot and pages 22–23 Apesteguy/Sipa/Rex Features.

Cuba and the Roots of Salsa: page 25 BBC (photo Michael Macintyre); pages 26–27 Kim Naylor/Link; page 27 David Browne; page 28 (top left) Julio Etchart; page 28 (top right) Redferns/David Redfern; page 28 (below left) David Browne; page 28 (below right) and page 31 (top) BBC (photo Michael Macintyre); page 31 (below) David Browne; page 33 Julio Etchart; pages 34–35 Kim Naylor/Link and page 37 Redferns/David Redfern.

New Country: page 39 Redferns/Simon Redfern; page 40 London Features International; page 42 Redferns/David Redfern; page 43 (centre) MCA Records; page 44 (top) Redferns/David Redfern; page 44 Warner Bros and page 46 MCA Records.

Rai: page 49 Adrian Boot; pages 51, 52 and 53 Jak Kilby; page 54 Trevor Herman; page 57 (top) Jak Kilby and page 57 (below) Adrian Boot.

World Music Mining: page 61 Islands Records; page 63 Redferns/Tim Hall; page 64 Sterns (photo J. M. Birraux) and page 65 Redferns/Tim Hall.

The Music of West Africa: page 69 BBC (photo Robert Hill); pages 70–71, 72 (top & below), 75 (centre) and 76–77 Jak Kilby; page 77 (inset) BBC (photo Spike Watson).

The Music of Hungary and Bulgaria: page 79 Interfoto MTI & Hungary (photo Károly Gink); pages 80–81 and 81 (top) Popperfoto; page 82 Mansell Collection; pages 83 and 84–85 G. D. Hackett; page 85 (top) Tim Sharman; page 85 (below) Hannibal Records; page 86 (centre) Tim Sharman; page 86 (below) Marco Vercruysse and page 87 (top & below) Hannibal Records.

Latin American Music and Politics: page 89 Associated Press; page 91 Alfredo Troncosa; pages 92–93 Julio Etchart; page 94 Joan Jara, via Frances Brown; page 95 (top) Alfredo Troncosa; pages 96–97 Associated Press and page 97 Popperfoto.

The Music of South Africa: page 99 BBC; pages 100–101 Popperfoto; pages 101 (top) and 102 (top) Virgin Records; page 103 David Browne; pages 102–103 Popperfoto; pages 104–105 Orde Eliason/Link; page 106 BBC and page 107 Jak Kilby.

The New Blues: page 109 Jak Kilby; page 110 Robert Freeman; page 111 Redferns/David Redfern; page 112 (below) BBC; pages 113 and 114 Val Wilmer; page 115 Melody Maker/Giuseppe G. Pino; pages 116–117 Val Wilmer and page 117 Redferns/David Redfern.

Into the Hot: page 119 Harlingue/Collection Viollet; page 120 Erich Auerbach; page 121 London Features International; pages 122–123 Frank Driggs Collection; page 122 (inset) Hulton Deutsch Collection; pages 124–125 Orde Eliason/Link; page 125 (below) Adrian Boot; page 126 Jak Kilby and page 127 Mary Evans Picture Library.

MAP ON PAGES 6 & 7 BY EDANART.

Published by BBC Books,
A division of BBC Enterprises Ltd
Woodlands, 80 Wood Lane, London W12 0TT

First published 1989
Reprinted 1990
© BBC Books, Francis Hanly and Tim May 1989

ISBN 0 563 20790 6

Typeset in 11/14 Bodoni
by Butler & Tanner Ltd, Frome
Printed and bound in Great Britain by Butler & Tanner Ltd, Frome
Cover printed by Richard Clay Ltd, Norwich

CONTENTS

ACKNOWLEDGEMENTS

Francis Hanly and Tim May, the Editors, would like to thank: David Byrne, Ranking Miss P, Jill Evans, Bob Portway, Steve Jamison, Pete Wane, Tim Platt, Erica Duclos, Janice Clift, Annabel Yonge, Dennis Marks, Mark Kidel, Tricia Chacon, Kate Meynell, Colin Knijff, Trish Stephenson, Guy Crossman, Joyce Gentle, Lynda Featherstone, Paul Tothill, Warwick Gee, Andy Frain, Marc Marot, Jumbo Vanrenen, Michael Dobson, Diana Mansfield, Udyan Prasad, Michael Macintyre, Michael Dibb and John Paul Davidson.

Thanks also to Nigel Finch and Anthony Wall, Series Editors of *Rhythms of the World*, and everyone else who has worked on the programmes, Heather Holden-Brown, Cath Speight, Sarah Spalding and Julian Flanders at BBC Books, and to Frances Abraham and Jennie Karrach for their picture research.

Rick Glanvill would like to thank: Charles Easmon & The African Dawn Collective; Ginny Tapley; Jumbo Vanrenen; Sterns/Triple Earth; Graeme Ewens.

NOTES ON THE CONTRIBUTORS

JOE BOYD is best known as a music producer and head of Hannibal Records. He has been instrumental in the recording and promotion of 'world music', especially from Eastern Europe.

JENNY CATHCART is currently working on *Rhythms of the World* and is the author of *Hey You!*, the recently published biography of Senegalese singer Youssou N'Dour.

ROBIN DENSELOW is a reporter for BBC's *Panorama* and a regular contributor to the *Guardian*. His latest book *When The Music's Over: The Story of Political Pop* is published by Faber.

JAN FAIRLEY is a freelance journalist, writer and broadcaster. She edits *Popular Music* for the Cambridge University Press and is currently writing a book on Latin American music.

RICK GLANVILL is a contributor to the *Guardian*, *City Limits*, *International Musician* and *ID* magazine. He broadcasts on the World Service and UK radio.

ROB PRINCE is a columnist for *Top* magazine and a feature writer for *Folk Roots*. He also broadcasts regularly for the BBC's World Service.

CHRIS STAPLETON is a freelance writer and journalist. He is the co-author of *African All-Stars* and has appeared on UK radio.

SUE STEWARD, journalist, television researcher, and sometimes DJ, is currently writing *Oye! Salsa!* for Thames and Hudson.

PHILIP SWEENEY is a writer and journalist who has specialised in 'world music'. He contributes regularly to the *Independent*, the *Guardian*, and the *Observer*.

ADAM SWEETING is a freelance writer and journalist who contributes on a regular basis to the *Guardian*.

DAVID TOOP is the author of *The Rap Attack: African Jive to New York Hip-Hop*. He is a regular columnist for *The Face* magazine.

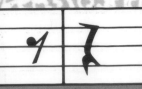

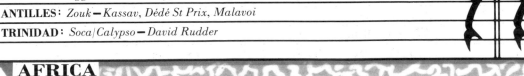

CARIBBEAN

5 **JAMAICA:** *Reggae — Bob Marley, Peter Tosh, Lee 'Scratch' Perry, Gregory Isaacs*

6 **ANTILLES:** *Zouk — Kassav, Dédé St Prix, Malavoi*

7 **TRINIDAD:** *Soca/Calypso — David Rudder*

AFRICA

8 **ALGERIA:** *Rai — Cheb Khaled, Cheb Mami, Chaba Fadela, Cheb Sahraoui, Chaba Zahouania*

9 **SENEGAL:** *Mbalax — Youssou N'Dour; Toure Kunda, Baaba Maal*

10 **MALI:** *The Griot Tradition — Salif Keita, Toumani Diabate, Kasse Mady,*
Zani Diabate and the Super Djata Band

11 **GUINEA:** *Mory Kante, Bembeya Jazz*

12 **IVORY COAST:** *African Reggae — Alpha Blondy*

13 **GHANA:** *Highlife — George Darko*

14 **SIERRA LEONE:** *Palm wine music — S.E. Rogie,*
Kwaa Mensah

15 **CAMEROON:** *Makossa — Manu Dibango*

16 **NIGERIA:** *Afrobeat — Fela Kuti; Juju — Sunny Ade, Ebenezer Obey, Dele Abiodun; Fuji — Kollington, Barrister*

17 **ZAIRE:** *Soukous and Rumba — Franco, Tabu Ley, Papa Wemba, Kanda Bongo Man, Zaiko Langa Langa*

18 **ZIMBABWE:** *Chimurenga — Thomas Mapfumo, Stella Chiwese, Oliver Mutukudzi; The Bhundu Boys, The Four*

19 **SOUTH AFRICA:** *Mbaqanga — Mahlathini and the Mahotella Queens, Soul Brothers;* *Brothers*
Johnny Clegg, Sipho Mabuse, Sipho Mchune, Malombo, Hugh Masekela

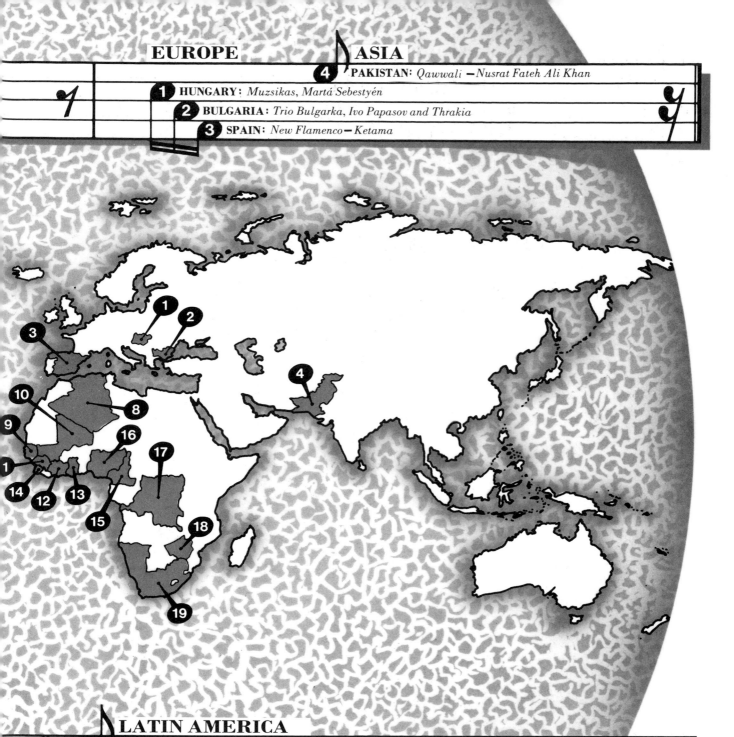

EUROPE   ASIA

4 PAKISTAN: *Qawwali — Nusrat Fateh Ali Khan*

1 HUNGARY: *Muzsikas, Martá Sebestyén*

2 BULGARIA: *Trio Bulgarka, Ivo Papasov and Thrakia*

3 SPAIN: *New Flamenco — Ketama*

LATIN AMERICA

20 CUBA: *Los Van Van, Celina Gonzalez, Orquestra Reve, Silvio Rodriguez, Carlos Puebla*

21 VENEZUELA: *Salsa — Oscar De Leon*

22 COLOMBIA: *Salsa — Joe Arroyo*

23 DOMINICAN REPUBLIC: *Merengue — Johnny Ventura, Wilfredo Vargas*

24 BRAZIL: *Samba and Fusions — Milton Nascimento, Caetano Veloso, Gilberto Gil*

25 ARGENTINA: *New Song — Mercedes Sosa, Atahualpa Yupanqui; Nuevo Tango — Astor Piazzolla;*
Rock Nacional — Charly Garcia, Victor Heredia

26 PANAMA: *Salsa — Ruben Blades*

27 CHILE: *Victor Jara, Violeta Parra, Inti Illimani*

28 NEW YORK: *Salsa — Celia Cruz, Tito Puente, Willie Colon, Ray Barretto, Johnny Pacheco*

29 PUERTO RICO: *Jibaro — Yomo Toro*

30 MIAMI: *Latin Hip-Hop — TKA, Miami Sound Machine, The Cover Girls*

31 SOUTHWEST LOUISIANA/LAFAYETTE: *Creole — Buckwheat Zydeco, Clifton Chenier, Queen Ida*

32 MISSISSIPPI DELTA: *Country/Acoustic Blues — Son House, Lightnin' Hopkins,*
Leadbelly, Robert Johnson, Howling Wolf

33 CHICAGO: *Electric Blues — Muddy Waters, B.B. King, Elmore James*

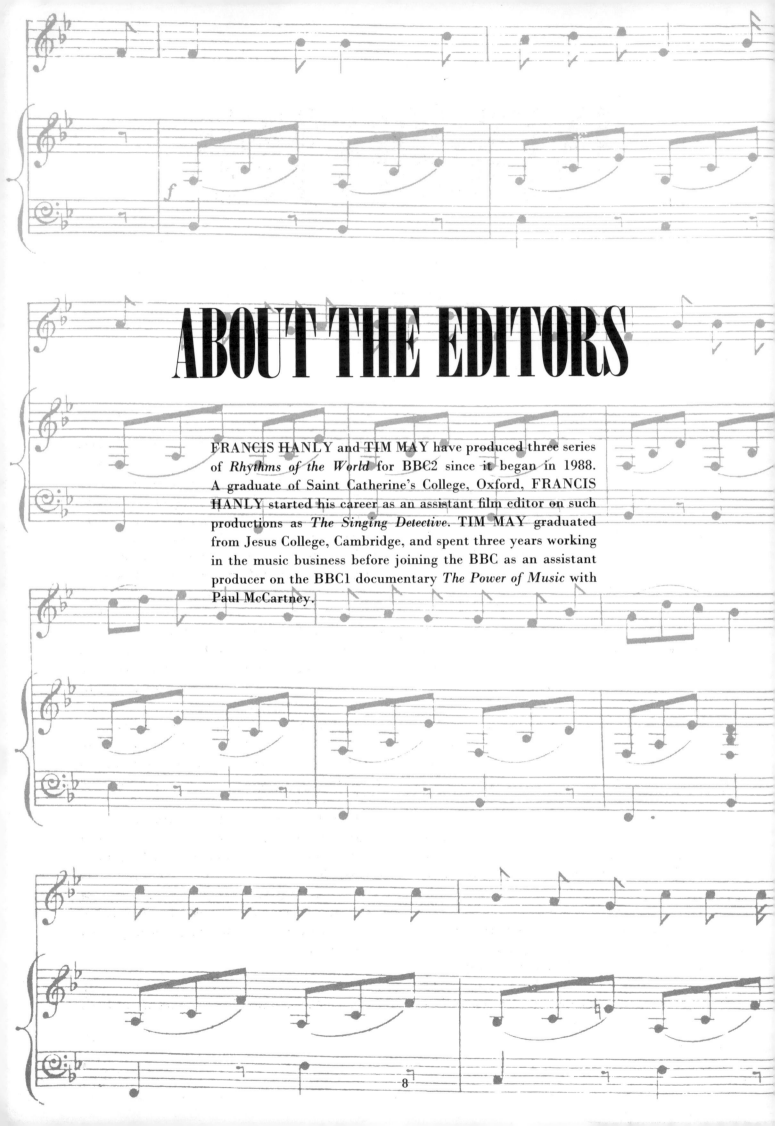

ABOUT THE EDITORS

FRANCIS HANLY and TIM MAY have produced three series of *Rhythms of the World* for BBC2 since it began in 1988. A graduate of Saint Catherine's College, Oxford, FRANCIS HANLY started his career as an assistant film editor on such productions as *The Singing Detective*. TIM MAY graduated from Jesus College, Cambridge, and spent three years working in the music business before joining the BBC as an assistant producer on the BBC1 documentary *The Power of Music* with Paul McCartney.

INTRODUCTION

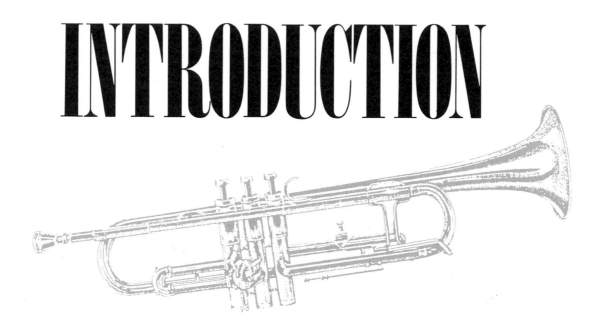

A couple of years ago, the term 'world music' entered our vocabulary – a neat marketing label for the faraway music with strange sounding names that was finding an audience over here. During the late 80s, rock and pop have become increasingly predictable and nostalgic and an appetite has developed for stronger stuff. If further proof were needed, several leading rock performers, notably Paul Simon, Peter Gabriel and David Byrne, have put new life into their own music by working with artists like Ladysmith Black Mambazo, Youssou N'Dour and Celia Cruz.

These artists have always been stars in their own worlds – it seems that our world is now ready for them. Times have changed. I remember seeing the Fania All-Stars at the Lyceum in 1974 – a representative of the sophisticated press told me that they 'sounded like Edmondo Ros'. Past attempts to introduce the music of Africa, Latin America and India have failed but this time it looks like it is here to stay.

Rhythms of the World developed out of *Arena* as a response to the phenomenon. On *Arena* we've always recognised the importance of music from the developing world, from the Carifesta of 1981, through Caribbean Nights and Bob Marley to Celia Cruz last year. But *Arena* has a broad brief for the arts and a new series was required. The styles of music are as various as the nations of the world and the regions within them – but the same spirit informs them all. Hugh Masekela recognised this

and said so in an *Arena* profile a few years ago: 'Mbaqanga became mbaqanga in the same way calypso became calypso, high life became high life in West Africa – or the way reggae became reggae in Jamaica. The way salsa became salsa to the Latins in the Caribbean. The way the samba is the samba in Brazil. In other words, it's the favela or the ghetto music of the under privileged classes.'

This book is intended to be a companion to the series. So far, *Rhythms of the World* has been performance based to present as much of the music as possible and as many of the prominent names. The book is an attempt to get behind the hype and address some of the issues raised by the recent explosion in 'world music'. The term itself makes sounds and places that were remote seem more accessible but at the same time it has to be more than a marketing tag. 'World music' raises serious questions about the relationship between the Third World and the First.

All of the contributors to this book are established commentators in the field, writers who can put the music into its context. Some of these apparently new sounds come from musical traditions stretching back centuries. *Rhythms of the World*, the book, aims to develop a debate on the most exciting thing that has happened in popular music this decade.

Anthony Wall,
Series Co-Editor *Arena* and *Rhythms of the World*

PARIS, AFRICA

CHRIS STAPLETON

Mamadou Konte, Salif Keita's manager in Paris, stretches himself to his full six foot something and says, 'You British, you were the first to explore, but now you have been passed by.'

Konte works from a small office in Pigalle. For ten years he has organised African concerts and festivals and in those ten years he has seen the growth of an African and black cultural movement that has left its stamp on the city – and helped forge a new relationship between the one-time colonisers and their former subjects.

Konte has a phrase for it. 'The Europeans colonised us,' he says. 'Now we've come to Europe.

Not to colonise but to civilise.'

The signs of this civilising process are already abundant. At Pigalle Underground station, the video screens hanging above the platform switch suddenly from the adverts to a film of Zaire's greatest band, Zaiko Langa Langa, playing in Paris the following week. In the backstreets of Barbes, Senegalese restaurants rub shoulders with West African tailors' shops and music stores whose racks of Algerian, Moroccan and Egyptian cassettes spill out onto the pavement. Tune to Nova FM and Rick James, Kassav, the Jungle Brothers and Alpha Blondy ride the airwaves. And then there is Tchico Tchicaya, from the Congo, with his current hit. The title: 'L'Ambience à Paris'.

(Opposite) Youssou N'Dour

Tchico has yet to reach the French charts, but others have. Senegalese band Toure Kunda led the way with their live Celluloid double album of 1984 which went gold with sales of 100 000. The studio album *Natalia* followed suit. Alpha Blondy's Ivory Coast reggae classic, 'Jerusalem', went gold for Pathé Marconi (EMI) in 1987. The following year, the laurels were shared between Mory Kante, a Guinean kora player whose glossily produced Barclay single 'Ye Ke Ye Ke' hit the top five and sold over 250 000 copies, with the album *Akwaba Beach* going gold; and Johnny Clegg and Savuka who had three months at the top of the album charts with their Zulu rock album *Third World Child* and reached number three with 'Shadow Man'.

The music of the Antilles – French-speaking West Indies – has also made its mark. Kassav, the pioneers of zouk, had their first gold with *Zouk La Se Sel Medikaman Nou Ni* in 1983, and signed to CBS four years later. In 1988, lead singer Jocelyne Beroard and white Martiniquan Phillipe Lavil reached number two in the singles chart with a re-cut of Kassav's 'Kole Serie'. Now there is the final accolade: a range of cosmetics bearing the Kassav imprint.

Away from the lotions and gold discs there are other, underground sounds which rarely reach the general public. Algerian rai music (described in Chapter 4) fuels a bustling Paris scene, which revolves around community dances and functions and a fast-selling cassette market; annual sales total over 50 000 in Paris alone. Although French producers and companies are now showing an interest, rai retains its own closely guarded identity.

Live music is also a largely underground, community affair, with top artists like Malavoi from the Antilles or Cheb Khaled, the king of rai, playing to packed suburban halls with little or no advertising. A couple of small posters under the bridge at Barbes announce a gig by Zairean singer Koffi Olomide; two nights later the place is packed. At The Dimension, a cavernous Montreuil basement, zouk artists like Eric Brouta and the robot-hipped Francky Vincent rock a 2000-strong crowd. The backing tapes wind to a halt at 5am. Album tracks take over, soukous and zouk keep the floor full till 7am.

Equally frantic is the studio scene, where African and Antillean artists turn out an assembly-line flow of Zairean soukous, zouk, Camerounian makossa, and all the mixtures in between; makozouk, soukozouk, you name it.

Until recently, few of the records would have found their way into the mainstream, but now larger stores like Fnac and the Virgin Megastore are carrying stock. One of the key distributors is Melodie, part of the Celluloid company, which distributes work from about ten small tropical music labels. A successful album, according to promotion manager François Post, will sell 10 000 and above to the African or Antillean market. *Super K*, Diblo's frenetic soukous work-out, shifted 12 000; the follow-up, *Soukous Trouble*, 15 000. *Moyibi*, by fellow Zaireans Pepe Kalle and Nyboma sold over 10 000.

To take the music further and promote the artists actively in the white market is another matter, as Bruno Barre at Blue Silver has found. The company works in three main areas: French music; Antillean with Malavoi and Dédé St Prix; and rai, the main artists being Cheb Mami an Cheb Kader. Barre agrees that Kassav have led the way in promoting zouk music – but a lack of media exposure makes it hard to take other artists beyond the black music scene. Half the white families of France may have a Kassav album, he explains, but when zouk bands play live the audience is almost totally Antillean.

Rai has met a different problem. After Oran, Paris is the music's second capital, but the racism directed at the North African communities makes it hard to promote rai with any success. Barre recalls the fuss surrounding the release of Cheb Kader's first Blue Silver album, which was taken off the FM stations after complaints from 'middle-aged racists'.

Celluloid, who first broke Toure Kunda on the

(Above) Mory Kante, one of the first African musicians in Paris to break into the mainstream

المجلس الشعبي البلدي

الجمعية الثقافية لمدينة وهران

Mercredi 3 Août 1988 A 21 h.

THEATRE DE VERDURE

GRANDE SOIRÉE

✳ ✳ RAÏ ✳ ✳

avec

Chabs
Mami
Tahar
Abdelhak

Chaba
Sabrina
Chab
Houari Benchenet

(Background) Place du Gouvernement, Algiers. (Top) Toure Kunda and (bottom) Kanda Bongo Man

French market, are now actively promoting Kanda Bongo Man from Zaire. François Post explains why they chose him; Bongo Man will turn up for press interviews, he is willing to write shorter songs for French pop consumption, to change his music to suit prevailing tastes, and to get away from what Post describes as the Zairean norm: 'Seven or eight minute songs talking about people who have helped the artists – or who can help them.'

A key figure in raising standards in Paris is Ibrahima Sylla, a Senegalese producer whose Syllart label has given a distinctive and sophisticated edge to recordings by Ismael Lo from Senegal, Mali's Salif Keita, Les Quatre Etoiles from Zaire and many others. Sylla has become successful by adopting rigorous business methods. His productions are legendary for the care and money – upwards of £40 000 in some cases – lavished on them. Sylla uses top studios, musicians and musical arrangers to take his Paris productions into the international league. He recoups his production costs – and pre-empts the pirates – by first releasing his album in Africa on cassette before putting out the records in Europe.

Such a vibrant scene may puzzle British observers accustomed to looking to Manchester, Liverpool, Chicago – at a pinch Kingston, Jamaica – for everything that moves and shakes. But Paris?

In fact black musicians – whether jazz, reggae or, as far back as the twenties, biguine and mazurka – have been a regular part of the city's life. In 1970, Zaire's Tabu Ley appeared at the Olympia and on French television, in a symbolic gesture that Africa's time had come.

The crucial link lies in the colonial past which saw the French flag planted from Algeria to the Antilles, down through West Africa to the Congo – now Congo Brazzaville. Colonial subjects were taught French language and culture; and the educated minorities were taught to think of themselves as French in a way that was rarely encouraged by the more cautious and parsimonious British.

With independence, former colonial subjects settled in the French 'motherland', while France kept up a flow of people, money and business to the former colonies. A strong link, at times suggestive of neo-colonial control, persisted, and musicians were to benefit accordingly.

For them Paris has two advantages; the studios are good and money can be moved easily to and fro. Apart from Guinea and Mauritania, all of France's former African colonies are part of the Franc zone. Martinique, Guadeloupe, and French overseas 'departments' use francs, while African states use the CFA which is tied to the French currency. There are few of the restrictions on taking money in and out of the country that affect citizens of former British colonies like Ghana and Nigeria.

The result has been that black producers can function with a certain ease in Paris. Throughout the seventies, immigration attracted little of the British-style backlash, and Africans felt generally welcome in the city. As one musician explains, 'Even today, there is none of the tension between the French and their blacks that you feel in Britain.'

The size of the market – France has over 4 000 000 immigrants, something like a third of them from North and West Africa – add to the attractions of working in the capital.

In the seventies African musicians, many of them Zaireans, came to Paris, recorded and carried records back home. Manu Dibango broke out of the ghetto briefly with his 1973 hit 'Soul Makossa', which won a wider audience. By the end of the decade though, the African scene was becoming too big to stay hidden. Partly through its own size and energy – and partly through an abrupt shift in French politics – African and black music became part of the overground life of the city.

Says producer Martin Meissonnier:

It was a fascinating period. Fela Kuti played his first French concert on 15 March 1981. Mitterrand came to power on 10 May 1981. This was a big change. When Fela played, suddenly people realised that here was an African guy who could fill a hall with 10 000 people. Record companies couldn't believe a guy could get so much publicity and be an African. As a result, musicians living in Paris became far more confident and we had a different period for the arts.

One of the first great changes of the Mitterrand era was the freeing of the airwaves which led to the creation, in the first three months, of thirty

(Over page left) Africans in Paris, 1935 and (over page right) African soldiers with their French officer, First World War

Paris VHF stations outside state control. A month later the figure had virtually quadrupled, bringing in a tide of stations representing every shade of musical taste. Since then numbers have fallen, but the FM stations, led by Nova, Tropic and Oui, continue their invigorating stream of soukous, funk, hip-hop, and reggae, alongside music from Mali and Guinea, and the latest zouk from the Paris studios.

The French Ministry of Culture has played a key role in the growth of the African scene. The name on most people's lips is Jack Lang who, as Minister of Culture from 1981, operated as a kind of Mr Fixit, helping African musicians with immigration and financial problems; appearing at Fela concerts; or helping Algerian rai singer Cheb Khaled with his papers. Mory Kante, Salif Keita and Papa Wemba all benefited from Lang's interventions. 'At one time,' says French journalist Hélène Lee, 'when there was a problem, the first question was "Do you have Jack Lang's telephone number?"'

The government put money into large French festivals – Africa Fête, the festivals at Bourges and Angoulême – which popularised the work of Keita, Youssou N'Dour and other major talents, and sponsored African bands returning to tour the African continent.

Smaller projects also received help. François Post, of Celluloid, recalls how Jack Lang helped Toure Kunda with a subsidy when money ran low, and helped with government finance for their first video. 'I remember him coming to a concert of theirs in 1983. The very fact that Jack Lang was there meant that the press and television both picked up on it.'

The interest in tropical music chimed with the growth of the human rights movement in France. SOS Racisme, the anti-racist organisation, brought African and Antillean bands to the forefront in the same way that Rock Against Racism had promoted reggae bands in Britain. In 1988 SOS Racisme's greatest coup, a three-way television spectacular linking Paris, Dakar and New York, brought music by Johnny Clegg, Dédé St Prix, the Wailers, Baaba Maal and Kanda Bongo Man to a vast television audience.

In 1984 the Parisian 'Band-Aid' single, 'Tam Tam Pour L'Ethiope', showed the extent to which

(Opposite) Manu Dibango – Big Blow

18

(Background) The young people of Paris at an SOS Racisme rally. (Top) Alpha Blondy. Ivory Coast reggae star. (Bottom) Dédé St Prix and (opposite) Ray Lema, originally from Zaire, now based in Paris

African artists, Mory Kante, Salif Keita, Souzy Kasseya from Zaire, and Toure Kunda, were now working together, rather than in separate national groupings. The same spirit pervaded the Jericho project, in which Keita and Konte joined members of Xalam from Senegal, and Ghetto Blaster, an Afrobeat band, to campaign for the release of Fela Kuti, then imprisoned in Nigeria.

One musician who played an important role in both was Ray Lema, the Zairean keyboards player. 'Since 1982 things have changed quickly in Paris,' he explains.

> French people are now far more aware of our presence. The government supports us because they feel that the French language is receding in the world and that French artists are unable to carry the language overseas. The Africans are the people who can do this – suddenly they are pushing us.

Lema caught the eye of officialdom with his *Bwana Zoulou Gang* album which featured several top musicians – playing, says Lema, not for any cause, but out of friendship. This led to a government proposal that Lema assemble an African-French touring supergroup.

But the government is not alone in its push for black music. The media have also been crucial, one of the more influential magazines being the monthly *Actuel*. The director, Jean-François Bizot, explains that the new 'sono mondiale' – or world sound – both reflects the new music being made in Paris and offers a direct challenge to a French music scene dominated by British and American multinationals. Bizot says:

> In Paris we've consumed British and American music since Piaf died. We got the impression more and more that we were musically undeveloped. Ten years ago, when punk came up, we were faced by yet another overseas fashion and we were wondering if Paris would ever amount to anything again.

Bizot, who set up Radio Nova, joined with sympathetic producers and musicians to explore the black cultural scene that was developing on their doorsteps. Of the major musical capitals – London, New York and Los Angeles – Paris seemed unique. Where London showed little interest in its bhangra and reggae, and New York was less a melting plot than a collection of separate musical tribes, Paris offered the chance to forge a musical common ground between the black and Middle-Eastern communities.

Actuel ran stories on Zairean music, then rai. At the Rex Club, African and New York punk bands played to diverse and puzzled crowds while Ray Lema, with help from Bizot, started work on a sound that could be danced to by blacks and whites. The first fruit was Lema's *Kinshasa-Washington DC-Paris* album; the second, *Medecine*, was produced by Martin Meissonnier.

However, popularising sono mondiale was fraught with problems. If Bizot and friends wanted to 'make a hole in white culture', the record companies seemed strongly resistant to the idea. Most of the majors in Paris are subsidiaries of British and American conglomerates with little interest in discovering new musics and mixtures.

Martin Meissonnier explains:

> I went to every French company trying to sell them Ray Lema and Salif Keita. But no company would take them. People like CBS are very shy. Virgin is a slave to the UK company. They're scared of signing up anyone. The only company that did anything good was Polygram with Mory Kante.

Kante's story offers an object lesson in popularising an African artist through the use of strong video, a highly commercial production – with what Ray Lema calls a 'white sound' – and the kind of tightly organised schedule of television appearances, interviews and concerts usually associated with major rock acts. Much of the early push came from Kante – who remains avid in his wish to conquer the world market – and Philip Constantin of Barclay, the Polygram subsidiary that gave Kante his greatest success. Breaking Kante, wrote Philippe Conrath in *Le Nouvel Observateur*, took *une mise de départ* (an opening stake) of 3 000 000 francs and 'three years of intelligent forcing'.

With Johnny Clegg and Savuka the hard graft was taken on not by Clegg's record company, EMI, but by the French management company, Claud 6. According to Claud 6's Bruno Bulay, EMI only threw their weight behind Clegg after his sensational French tour of 1988.

The contrast with London could not be more acute. Clegg fell foul of a Musicians' Union ban. Mory Kante's 'Ye Ke Ye Ke' came out in three different mixes to the confusion of record buyers. French music industry people accuse the British of being too 'purist' in their tastes. Show them Toure Kunda and they want something more 'ethnic'. Show the wider public something sung in a foreign language and they want English. In France pop music is often sung in a foreign language. The British don't have a 'world sound' – they just have record companies.

Yet there are other differences. Why do so few Anglophone musicians from Ghana or Nigeria settle in Britain – in the way the Francophone artists have in France? Ghanaian journalist Kwabena Fosu-Mensah explains that coming into Britain from West Africa is a hassle, that public interest in African music is well below the level needed to tempt the more established artists, and that British political institutions have shown a less than welcoming face to black immigrants.

'Also British media and the industry tend to overrate the musicians coming in on tour,' he says. 'And because respect and credibility is given to musicians from the outside, there is little point in Anglophone musicians coming to settle here.'

Despite this, British companies have given a kind of perverse encouragement to French companies – and musicians – by rushing to sign acts based in Paris. Laurent Viguie, owner of the Cannibal production company, says:

A lot of people in Paris were mystified when Island signed Salif Keita. Now French companies have seen people signing to British ones – Youssou N'Dour to Virgin, a lot of my bands to Island – and they have decided that something ought to be done about it.

In general, British journalists have an overblown idea of Paris. The bands are here, yes, but because they are Francophile, it's the obvious place to come. But in business terms, look at how many of our bands are signed to the majors ...

Jean-François Bizot takes a more optimistic view:

We had the Anglo-Saxon colonisation – and the only way we could get out of that was to prove that we could export something from France. We couldn't do it with French music. Sono mondiale was the way to break the monopoly of black music from America – and of rock from the UK. The British may be buying up our bands – but at least they are now actually buying something here ...

Talk of Paris as the centre of black music is premature. Its strength however lies in the new sounds born from a creative meeting of artists from Africa, the Antilles, and beyond. Check any zouk album, and the chances are that Zairean guitarists will be playing on it. Check the new soukous for a dose of sprightly, zouk-style percussion. The new Salif Keita album has a French producer and a Camerounian arranger. Producer Martin Meissonnier has just finished an album featuring Tunisian singer Amina plus Turkish musicians, Zairean drummer Boffi and a Congolese keyboard player. 'This is a city where musicians speak to each other,' he explains.

The result is a polyglot musical culture where new formations – the pan-African high-tech of Salif Keita's *Ko-Yan*, the lavishly arranged sounds of Kasse Mady or Papa Wemba – are putting to rest the old stereotype of an endlessly cheerful upbeat tropical sound – 'sun and palm tree' music. For musicians, Paris is crucial. As Ray Lema says:

Before, there was a jazz tribe, a reggae tribe, a rock tribe. Now we are at a turning point where people can play anything – but without that frame of mind that says 'This is jazz, this is funk ...' I say to a musician, 'Here's the bridge, I want it to sound rock, or jazz or zouk,' and they can do it, immediately. That's why I feel excited here.

The city offers a platform for African and Antillean musicians plus a chance of further world exposure. But it also spells, for Mamadou Konte, a shift in social attitudes. Says Konte:

Colonisation is finished. We are living in a period of change, when people are coming together. In

(Background) Place Pigalle

France we have discovered a flexibility in the political structure – and have worked to create a mix of cultures. In ten to twenty years, Paris will be the European centre of black music.

CUBA AND THE ROOTS OF SALSA

SUE STEWARD

As Gorbachev flew into Havana for his first meeting with Fidel Castro, just 100 miles away in Downtown Miami, the Kiwani Society were issuing statements from the Little Havana office, about the banning of musicians from their annual salsa carnival in Calle Ocho. Some popular artists, including the Brazilian Denise do Kalase and Puerto Rican salsa bandleader Andy Montanez were on the list. Montanez's crime had been a visit – in 1979 – to Cuba on a cultural exchange. There were outcries, of course. Montanez and his salsa orchestra had stolen the show the previous September in Madison Square Garden's annual

salsa festival; every song had driven the 20 000 Hispanics in the audience wild. The ban was highy controversial but the Kiwanis are Miami Cubans, and that means any sign of familiarity with the Castro regime is anathema to them.

This single event crystallises the political rift which runs through salsa today. Although it is thirty years since the Revolution, the dust has not settled. The subject of Cuban music still raises blood pressures. Whilst it is undeniable that music from Cuba forms the rootstock of all that is now known as salsa, salsa has developed an independent identity throughout Latin America and in the USA (Miami and New York are the most

(Opposite) Jorge Reyes, bass player with Cuban trumpeter Arturo Sandoval

RHYTHMS OF THE WORLD

significant urban centres).

Thirty years ago, the American blockade stemmed the flow of music from Cuba into New York's dance halls and recording studios, and from there into the rest of the world then in the throes of chachacha and mambo madness. Since then, salsa music, the popular dance music of Latin Americans (except the Brazilians, who have their own quite different history and identity), has changed and been modernised, but is still structurally the same.

The term 'salsa' was first used in the early nineteen-seventies. The bosses of the emergent Fania Records label, Jerry Masucci and Johnny Pacheco, appropriated the term from enthusiasts who shouted 'SALSA!' at a particularly 'cooking' soloist. Salsa actually means 'hot sauce'. Masucci and Pacheco were employing a classic marketing tactic – labelling a genre to help market it. What they were labelling was the sound of mostly New York-based, mostly Puerto Rican bandleaders (Pacheco is originally from the Dominican Republic, but Cuban music courses through his veins), who were building on the mambo, rumba, guaguanco, danzon, and other Cuban rhythms which had flooded the market before the Revolution. In the hands of this new breed of musicians in New York, the tempos were speeded up, instrumentation (especially the horns) became snappier, and new instruments and idioms were introduced from non-Cuban, particularly Puerto Rican, sources.

As a term, 'salsa' remains controversial. Musicians love to hate it, but use it all the same. Tito Puente said: 'It's meaningless, it could just as easily have been matsoh ball soup.' Daniel Ponce sang: 'I only think of salsa when I sit down to eat.' And the Cuban musicians rejected the term as a capitalist plot to exclude their music from the marketplace. Trumpeter Arturo Sandoval, on his first visit to London in 1985, claimed:

Salsa was invented by some clever people in America who wanted to block the Cubans out of the commercial market. With the word 'salsa', they were trying to promote the idea that it is modern, upmarket stuff and what is going on in Cuba now is passé.

Today, the term is universally accepted, but accepted as meaning little.

It is also agreed that the roots of salsa are divided between Spanish harmonies and song structures, and the Afro-Cuban rhythm known as 'son'. Son originated in the black sections of Cuba's eastern province of Oriente. It drew together elements from African music, dance and religious traditions retained from the days of slavery, and Spanish-descended song structures, in the rural style known as guajira. The originators were acoustic sextets, beautifully recalled in a two-album set, The Roots of Salsa, with music from Sextetos Habanero and Bolona. These records provide the perfect introduction to the fundamentals of salsa, being the equivalent of the early field recordings of African-American blues artists. For son, after all, is Cuba's blues.

In the sleeve notes, John Santos writes: 'The son is a result of the combination of stringed instruments . . . [and] African-derived rhythm elements.' Bongos, cowbells, maraccas, guiro and claves play the rhythms, while 'the anticipated feel of the string bass, played in pizzicato style, and the rhythmic strumming of the guitar are also signatures of the son.'

Musically, the basis is purely African – the montuno or estribillo (rhythmic sections of the song) offer opportunity for improvisation, and the call-and-response between the improvising lead singer and the chorus which repeats phrases, is a direct descendant from West African forms. Salsa merely modernised the line-up, extending to piano, conga, drums, horns and eventually electronic instruments.

Today, salsa is such an all-embracing and nebulous term, that it is easier to define it by saying what it is not. It is not Mexican mariachi, with its Mexican Indian background; nor is it Brazilian music with its Portuguese ancestry; nor again the Dominican Republic's merengue in 2/4 time; it is none of Columbia's rich rhythms – the porro, joroppo, and particularly the cumbia, which gives salsa such a run for its money in the clubs of Queens and Hialeah today. None of these fit the definition, however broad. Neither do the ballads, which currently have an entire chart to themselves in Billboard magazine, because salsa is primarily dance music.

The distinction between salsa and Latin jazz is a much finer one. In the hands of a virtuoso, salsa,

(Background) Havana, Cuba and (opposite) Daniel Ponce – Cuban born but based in New York

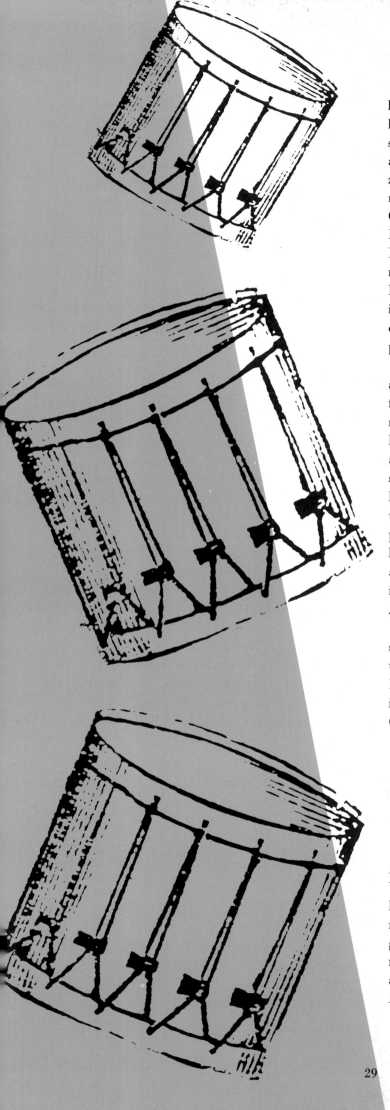

like jazz, relies on improvised solos, but most salsa bands these days play to charts and even the solos are prearranged. Moreover Latin jazz is itself another umbrella term, incorporating both Brazilian music and rock in the West Coast fusions of musicians like Airto and Carlos Santana, and Afro-Cuban experiments with bebop in the music of Paquito d'Rivera and his former Cuban band Irakere. There is also the eclectic range of inspiration (from classical music to modernists like McCoy Tyner), at work in the inspired meanderings of pianist Eddie Palmieri. None of these fit comfortably with a definition of salsa, but all are potent influences on it.

Salsa is as susceptible to the influence of fashion as any other kind of music, and this is as true for the instrumentation as it is for the musical nuances. Salsa orchestras switch and change their horns to suit the prevailing mood. The numbers and configurations of trumpet, trombone, and saxophone, rise and fall, creating fuller, funkier, harsher, or sweeter sounds according to the current trend. Predictably, in such a rhythm-based genre, percussionists are held in high esteem, and traded like soccer stars. New 'hard hands' create a buzz, and competitive 'cutting' contests in salsa clubs in New York are as popular as cockfights in San Juan.

Given the proliferation and cross-fertilisation of salsa styles over the last thirty years, it is both unfair and inaccurate to suggest the progress in Latin music has been limited to what happens inside Cuba. Yet hardline critics of salsa, like the Cuban percussionist Daniel Ponce still claim:

> When I came to America [in 1981] I said, 'Salsa! Yuk! this is old music.' I was expecting to find a stronger Latin scene here. Listen to Tito Puente and Machito from the nineteen-sixties and listen today. Different names but the music and the arrangements haven't changed.

Admittedly, inside Cuba, composers like Los Van Van's Juan Formell, and Irakere's Chucho Valdes, have turned the music inside out. The greatest risks and the most outrageous experiments are still going on behind the partially shut doors of Cuba's recording studios and nightclubs. Yet it could be argued that salsa composers and arrangers in America and elsewhere simply act in a more subtle

(Top left) Celina Gonzalez – leading exponent of the 'guajira' style. (Top right) Tito Puente. (Bottom left) Daniel Ponce – Salsa percussionist extraordinaire and (bottom right) Trumpeter and keyboards player Arturo Sandoval

29

and restrained fashion. And prejudice cuts both ways. Lack of easy access by American-based musicians accounts for much of their bias against modern Cuban music. They either take the same line as Celia Cruz that 'nothing interesting is happening there', or agree with Tito Puente that 'it's too clever, the music is too complicated and people can't dance to it. They're too far ahead of themselves.' Cuba's isolation has, until very recently, impeded the natural processes of absorption and cross-fertilisation which have been responsible for the incredible, fast-moving fusions at work elsewhere in the world music scene.

Inside Cuba, there have been other factors at work too. For example, the practice of sending young musicians to college has denied the music the intuitive raw talent which gave pre-Revolutionary music its fire. Many of the key characters in the reshaping of Cuban music in the early nineteen-seventies on the Fania label, were self-taught. Willie Colon, one of the most consistently important and eclectic arranger/composers, was a ghetto kid with a passion for trombones and dreams in his head. Johnny Pacheco, who co-owns Fania and has retained a central position in the salsa scene since the sixties, started playing harmonica in the Dominican Republic and learnt violin from his father.

But New York musicians like Pacheco have not had it all their own way. The domination of the New York-based orchestras has been threatened during the late eighties, as a new generation of Caribbean and South American artists have made inroads into the salsa scene. Venezuelan singer and bandleader Oscar D'Leon has achieved phenomenal success with his traditional-sounding reworkings of Cuban classics. D'Leon admits to mild eclecticism; he is not afraid to borrow from any number of sources. 'I use little jazzy beats, some African, Cuban, Puerto Rican influences ... What I've done is taken a little from everywhere ... like a chef.' The Colombian singer Joe Arroyo is typical of a confident new generation, aware of the difference between it and the American Latins, and open to music drifting in from the Caribbean, on radio and record. Zouk, merengue, and soca all influence his music. In the Dominican Republic, the spiritual home of merengue, new experiments are transforming this rather restricted rhythmic form.

Ramon Orlando's use of fresh arrangements for Orquesta Internationale and his incorporation of electronic instruments, and Luis Guerra's Juillard-trained ear and passion for Manhattan Transfer's smooth harmonies, mark them out as being among the most progressive of the new generation.

Under the guidance of musicians like Arroyo and Orlando, Latin music is entering a new era, characterised by divergence, experimentation, eclecticism and a fresh openness to other types of music. This openness is essential if Latin music is to continue to grow and to weather the criticism of being old-fashioned, kitsch, or sentimental. However, this sort of development carries its own risks. A new generation of young Latin Americans in the USA, the 'beans'n'rice and hamburger generation', to coin a Miami Sound Machine phrase, consider themselves to be Americans first and Latin Americans second, and their musical tastes reflect this. Salsa artists must keep their music exciting enough to rival the overwhelming popularity of American urban styles like rap and house music. Many young composers are responding by incorporating rock and rap elements into salsa, but even more are deserting the style altogether. Salsa is at a crucial point in its history.

Just as the popular music of most Third World countries today shows the benefits and the pitfalls of the new era of instant, global communication, so salsa artists are in the process of defining their future place in the scheme of international music. Meanwhile, non-Latin artists are rapidly discovering the glories of Latin music, and swiftly incorporating its rhythmic and instrumental ideas into their own compositions. In the light of this sort of dynamic musical exchange, the isolationist and nationalistic attitudes of Little Havana seem thankfully irrelevant.

Ruben Blades: crossover dreamer

Rudy Veloz lived in El Barrio. He sang in salsa bands and his mentor was an old Cuban singer who played congas. Rudy was also an American who lived a daily bilingual crossover life. He badly wanted to be an American rock star. After he successfully crossed the divide, made money through songs in English, and journeyed with

(Top) Los Van Van and dancers at the Tropical, Havana and (bottom) Irakere on one of their frequent trips to London

exploitative managers, betraying friends and watching his dreams dissolve, he returned to his old marginalised life, disillusioned.

Rudy Veloz is a mythical character, an archetype portrayed by that masterful creator of archetypal characters, Ruben Blades, in the movie *Crossover Dreams*. Ruben Blades is a crossover dreamer. In 1988 he released an album called *Nothing but the Truth*, which featured songs by Lou Reed, Sting, and Elvis Costello, sung in English, and clad in salsa-flavoured rock. Yet Ruben is smarter than Rudy -- more cautious, and more in control of his career because of his ability to analyse the music business and recognise not only the options open to him but also the pitfalls.

Ruben Blades is arguably salsa's most controversial figure. In any musical genre he would be exceptional, a kind of renaissance man who can fill a number of different roles with ease. In the deeply conservative world of Latin music, his radicalism is even more exceptional. And yet, in spite of his radical stance and unconventional way of doing things, ever since his arrival in New York from Panama in 1973, he has managed to maintain a central position in that most conservative of aristocracies, the New York salsa scene, focussed throughout the seventies and early eighties on Fania Records.

In 1985, Blades used Linda Rondstadt and Joe Jackson on his *Escenas* (*Scenes*) album. At the same time he was working for his Masters law degree at Harvard University. In 1989, Attorney Blades won the Grammy award for Latin artist of the year. Simultaneously, he was scooping up awards for his role in Robert Redford's *Milagro Beanfield War* in which he played Sheriff Bernabe Montoya in a peace-keeping role. In real life, Blades makes no secret of his unaligned left-wing politics, a political position which adds to his reputation as a renegade, and feeds numerous rumours about his involvement with organised politics. In Miami, where the Cubans campaign tirelessly against anyone seemingly left of centre, his records are banned by some radio stations and record stores. However, in Europe and large parts of Latin America, he is worshipped as a visionary

WILLIE COLON PRESENTS RUBEN BLADES

and praised for his anti-American, anti-imperialist views. Above all, he is loved for his perceptive and poetic song-writing.

The characters that inhabit Blades' songs could pass you in a Spanish Harlem street or sit beside you in a Little Havana bar. Vivid images of everyday life have become his trademark. Pedro Navajo (who is part of the best-selling salsa album ever *Siembra* – a collaboration with that other great barrio dreamer Willie Colon) and Pablo Pueblo (the fruit of another Blades/Colon writing partnership, *Metiendo Mano*), are now as familiar to Spanish-speakers as the faceless blue-collar heroes in the songs of Bob Dylan, Bruce Springsteen and Gil Scott Heron.

Pablo Pueblo – Mr Everyman Latin American style – is described by Blades as

The man who comes home from work in a factory, walks into the same neighbourhood with the same old half-torn political advertisements with half-smiling faces, promising new tomorrows. He goes into the same reality of the neighbourhood, same dog peeing on the corner, same music coming out of the jukebox, in the same bar where he goes to drown his sorrows on Saturdays and Sundays. He goes to his room where he sees his wife and children sleeping in the same bed he's gonna crawl into. And he thinks, 'How long is this gonna stand?'

Ideas like that blew fresh air through the tired salsa obsessions with dancing, romantic love and memories of pre-Revolutionary Cuba, long since lost to singers and audience alike. His work is not universally popular – people still need the reassurance of the familiar, the old-fashioned themes and tried and tested style of the majority of salsa's artists. Even in love songs, Blades' couples are realistically portrayed as anxious, awkward people trying to make sense of their lives, alone and together. Critics like to focus on the entertainment versus reality debate. Blades shrugs it off – and his records are million-sellers. 'I'm breaking away from the dancing scheme structures by saying that this music is not just for dancing,' he said, just prior to finishing *Escenas*.

I'm going to make music that is a commentary,

(Opposite) Ruben Blades

utilising any pattern, any rhythm any construction that I want. Forget dancing as the only way, but I'm not advocating the disappearance of dance music. We always want to dance. I'm only saying that music must also consider other needs.

Blades is not alone. The Panamanian dentist-turned-salsa-singer, Omar Alfanno, writes songs of similar social realism. Willie Colon, Blades' former partner, has shadowed his every new move – musically, thematically, in performance, sartorially. Blades has returned the compliment, though it is clear that since their separation in 1984, each has gradually developed a confident individual style. Colon's writing is altogether drier and more satirical, but his subjects are no less controversial. For his first crossover album *Criollo*, he chose Three Mile Island and Latin American generals as two of his themes, and orientated the album towards a new bright sound of Caribbean-influenced salsa. Musically, Colon seems much closer to the sound of the barrio than Blades. His 1986 salsa-rap single 'Set Fire to Me' is just one example of his attempts to utilise what he hears around him. While Blades has moved closer to rock and is credited more for his song lyrics, Colon continues to explore a wealth of musical styles, absorbing music from Brazil, the Caribbean, and white and black America.

We should also remember that in broad terms, Blades is working within a well-established song-writing tradition. In pre-Revolutionary Cuba, son, like merengue and calypso from neighbouring islands, dealt with real social issues. After the Revolution, the *nova trova* (new song) movement emerged, led by Pablo Milanes and Silvio Rodri-guez, which married traditional folk music to a lyrical treatment of social and political issues. Their work paralleled that of Chileans, Inti Illi-mani and Violeta Parra, and Brazilians, Caetano Veloso and Gilberto Gil. Many nova trova songs are today covered by salsa bands in Puerto Rico and New York – a sign that Cuba is not as isolated as many artists (both Cuban and New York-based) like to maintain. Los Van Van, Cuba's top dance band, often use their songs as vehicles for social comment. Their lyrics are turned into catch-phrases by the people and can be heard all over the island. Los Van Van's main songwriter Juan Formell is well aware of the influence they have:

'You can get away with a lot because it's music for dancing. But it also has to be lighthearted – it can't be too serious.'

At the Paris Olympia festival in 1986, Blades and Los Van Van shared the same bill – neutral territory – and joined forces on a stirring version of 'Muevete' ('Move Yourself'). This song, written by Los Van Van's Juan Formell and rewritten and rearranged by Blades, has become a rallying signature tune for thousands of Latin Americans.

From the Caribbean to Soweto in Africa, our song goes, saluting those who defend freedom and use truth as a shield
There's not a bullet that can kill truth when reason defends it
Let us join together to finish off evil.
Move and put your heart in it.

As the eighties draw to a close, Ruben Blades, consciously different and ever-willing to experiment and collaborate, has become a self-styled spokesman for unity, progress and change throughout Latin America.

Celia Cruz: divine diva

Salsa is a man's world. Its stages are crowded with self-styled specimens of macho manhood, keen not only to compete with each other but also to enjoy being part of a 'boys' club'. There's little room in this world for women, except as singers, and the sight of vibes-player Valerie Naranjo, in New York's salsa band Carabali, is truly exceptional. Each generation of Latin Americans is credited with producing honey-voiced, good-looking singers who create a style of their own or impart new meaning to the classic songs, but it is rare for these artists and innovators to be women.

The enormous popularity of the ballad tradition in the late eighties has increased the number of prominent female singers – but women singing innocuous love songs have never been a problem. The real skill lies in being able to tackle raunchy, up-tempo salsa with its complexities and compulsory ad-libs, and in being able to handle the dynamics of working with a large orchestra. A

(Background) Havana, Cuba

CUBA AND THE ROOTS OF SALSA

few women have made their mark: Luisa Maria Hernandez ('La India de Oriente') enjoyed success in Cuba before the Revolution and continued to record after moving to America after 1960. Afro-Cuban son and the rural guajira with its lyrical Spanish harmonies, became her forte. Celina Gonzalez, still a dedicated Revolutionary, is famous for her classic duet recordings with her husband, made in the fifties. She has become synonymous with the guajira style, and like La India also uses her songs as vehicles for tribute to the various saints of the Santeria cult religion. In Miami, Linda Leida looked as if she might become one of the greats, but was gunned down in the street by her lover before she really had a chance to shine.

Arabella, an exiled Colombian who now lives in Miami, also shows star potential. She has a fiery edge to her voice and an intuitive ability to improvise. Arabella has chosen the traditional Cuban son as a vehicle for her talent, but she will need all her skill and determination to topple the universally acknowledged queen of salsa, a woman who has occupied the throne for over three decades and shows no sign of flagging. For singers and audience alike, Celia Cruz, queen of salsa, has become an idol, a diva whose supremacy is beyond question.

A Celia Cruz performance is unforgettable – cathartic, purifying and invigorating. She seems to consume her audience body and soul, and is rumoured to receive her powers from the gods and shamans of the Santeria cult religion. Cruz denies this but the stories simply add to her mythical status.

For her fans, Celia Cruz has come to embody a whole range of feelings about Cuba and life in exile after the Revolution. Her own success in an alien culture inspires them, while her songs bring back warm memories of life in Old Havana. For the young, she provides a link with a past they never knew but are forever hearing about at home.

Recently, Cruz has shown signs of wanting to move away from her accepted place in the Latin American music scene. Willie Colon, her producer on albums like *The Winners* (1988), has encouraged her to experiment with different musical styles. 'Un bembe pa' yemya', an Afro-Cuban song for the goddess of the seas, is typical of the sort of material she was famed for in the fifties, but has been funkily arranged against a rap/rock-influenced salsa tune. On the soundtrack of Jonathan Demme's movie *Something Wild*, she and Talking Heads' rock star David Byrne sang a duet called 'Loco de amor'.

Such adventurousness in such a slow-moving medium is unusual. For a woman approaching seventy, it is extraordinary. Yet Celia Cruz seems to possess eternal youth. She can be a giggly, girlish flirt but the men who surround her treat her like a sister, a best friend – one of the boys. On stage, she delivers a performance of ferocious energy, as she skitters and sashays across the floor, chatting to the audience, urging on the musicians and singing to raise the roof.

Celia Cruz's career took shape in the late forties, after she entered a competition in Havana and won a fruit tart and a radio contract. She came to the attention of Rogelio Martinez who led the legendary Sonora Matancera. He took her on as part of his roadshow of singers, dancers and musicians and they travelled around Cuba and Latin America, playing live and recording songs which became the basis of her repertoire for many years. When Castro came to power, Sonora Matancera left Cuba and Cruz went too.

The music of Sonora Matancera is rooted in the Afro-Cuban tradition. It is heavily percussive and relies on rapport between singer and soloists. Celia Cruz soon revealed an extraordinary talent for ad-libbing and improvisation. Her ideas are delivered in a rapid stream with diamond precision. Johnny Pacheco, who has worked with Cruz since the early seventies, recalls his first audition with 'La Diva': 'She sang the song "Caramelo" and it was like watching a computer. She listed every tropical fruit you can imagine at a speed I couldn't believe.'

Working with Pacheco on the Fania label, Cruz achieved phenomenal solo success. In-house producers Willie Colon and Ray Baretto helped secure her position as the most famous, best-loved and most successful female Latin American singer of all time.

Today, Celia Cruz tours virtually non-stop. In 1988, she visited Japan and drove audiences there wild. Such is her power and charisma as a singer that literal communication seems to be irrelevant. Yet she can still walk down a Manhattan street, dripping in mink and diamonds, unrecognised except by the Latin Americans who take jobs in New York as doormen, messengers, cleaners and domestics. Above all, Celia Cruz belongs to them and it is with this audience that she really comes into her own.

(Opposite) Celia Cruz, Queen of Salsa

THE NEW COUNTRY SOUND

ADAM SWEETING

The only problem with 'new country' is that nobody knows what it is. A swift check uncovers influences including rock, folk, bluegrass, pop, rockabilly, big-band, western swing and blues. If you can detect a common link between artists as dissimilar as Steve Earle, Randy Travis, or Cajun hopeful Jo-El Sonnier, you may just be the person to discern the missing connection between ironing and nouvelle cuisine. Suffice to say that new country embraces the past, present and future of country music, and doesn't insist that you ride a horse.

The last four years or so have seen country making swift strides towards broad acceptance by audiences who might previously have thought that it was corny, sentimental and nothing to do with them. In Britain the annual festivals at Wembley have featured some of country's biggest acts, but at the same time have tended to reinforce the most woeful clichés of 'country and western', with middle-aged fans turning up in stetsons and bootlace ties to eat takeaway Mexican food.

Now, operations like Route 88 and its successor, ingeniously called Route 89, have established a batch of new-look country-orientated artists playing at more hospitable venues. Performers like Dwight Yoakam, Lyle Lovett, The Judds and

(Opposite) Emmylou Harris

Nanci Griffith have found rapidly growing acceptance from crowds which fit nobody's preconception of a 'country' audience. Rock fans, for instance, seem to be finding qualities in country music which rock has turned its back on.

Not that the idea of new country is all that new. Like most kinds of music, country has had its peaks and troughs. It hit a slump in the mid-sixties, when Beatles-type groups were all the rage. During the seventies, country was rescued from the petrified clutches of a host of ageing artists by the 'Outlaw' movement spearheaded by Willie Nelson and Waylon Jennings, who adopted some of the sounds and attitudes of rock to capture a young, hip audience.

The Outlaw tag was partly a shrewd piece of record company marketing, epitomised by RCA's 1976 compilation album, *Wanted: The Outlaws*. 'Everybody rushed to buy the Outlaws album,' recalled Tompall Glaser, one of the featured artists. 'Rock'n'rollers, kids, lockjaw types from the East, people who'd never bought a country album in their whole lives bought that album.' But there was a genuine spirit of progress in the air too, without which ground-breaking records like Willie Nelson's *Red Headed Stranger* could not have come about.

Among the changes wrought by the Outlaws, apart from a move towards longer hair and hints of a more liberal lifestyle among the country community, was a shift in the balance of power between artists and record companies. Henceforth, performers would be able to exercise greater control over their sound and their recordings, and a new generation of record producers rose to prominence in Nashville. Men like Billy Sherrill, Jack Clement, Jimmy Bowen and Chips Moman moved into the recording studios, bringing with them a musical scope and a sense of adventure often lacking in their predecessors like Chet Atkins or Owen Bradley.

By the late seventies, country music had burgeoned into a $500 000 000-a-year industry, but even as it grew to embrace an increasing percentage of American record buyers, it inevitably became smoother around the edges, and records were sweetened to ensure mass appeal. By the early eighties, country had relapsed into the doldrums of syrupy production and bland material. Encouraged by the media boom surrounding the John Travolta picture, *Urban Cowboy*, which saw rhinestones and stetsons sprouting from Wall Street to Rodeo Drive while discos hastily reformatted to incorporate country music, the Nashville record labels had gone off in pursuit of the chart mainstream, with the stuff American radio programmers like to call 'adult contemporary'.

Disgruntled country fans and performers were becoming aware of the need for another new broom to unclog the airwaves and the recording studios. Emmylou Harris, erstwhile musical partner of the doomed but hugely influential country-rocker Gram Parsons, is widely credited with being one of a tiny handful of artists who kept the flame of 'true' country alive during this period of drastic bland-out. She remembers the era without enthusiasm.

> There was this incredible stampede to cross over. If you turned on the radio, you didn't know if you had the easy-listening station or the country station. You used to hear the term 'too country', and you heard it a lot. It used to make me sick! What were they talking about?

This time, the solution was less clear-cut than it had been a decade or more earlier, and involved a disparate cast of performers reaching back to country's multiple roots. Fortunately for fans of the real thing, most of them would be considered 'too country' for the Urban Cowboy era. Somehow, though, they were able to achieve substantial record sales too.

It's safe to say that the stars of new country are sticklers for traditional values. They like their country neat, and the country audiences love them for it. Some of the most successful of them, like George Strait, Grammy-grabbing Randy Travis and Reba McEntire, have travelled in the opposite

(Above) Johnny Cash

direction from Nelson and Jennings. They've achieved success by reviving the 'pure' country sound of George Jones or Tammy Wynette, which had become blurred under swathes of schmaltz and strings.

Hence, George, Randy and Reba have sometimes been packaged under the paradoxical heading of 'New Traditionalist', which is a little like being tagged as a Young Fogey. 'I think the country music audience was always out there, I just think they weren't gettin' that kind of music from the radio stations,' was how Strait put it, with characteristic Texan brevity.

Strait has become the matinée idol of country's new dawn, a cowboy who really does rope steers in Texas when he has time off. At least one commentator has already proposed George as the natural heir to the singing cowboys like Roy Rogers or Gene Autry, who went down big with movie audiences in the thirties and forties.

As for Randy Travis, maybe he could be the new Jim Reeves, with his lop-sided grin and air of immense relaxation. To hear Randy sing a song like 'Digging Up Bones' is to be reminded of the meaning of casual. Travis, a short-order cook in a Nashville restaurant until recently, is another Southern boy who learned from an early age to take his country music straight. 'It got for a while where if it hadn't been for Merle Haggard and George Jones, you wouldn't have heard much of the type of country music that we're doing,' Randy pondered, his vowels rolling over on their backs to have their tummies tickled. 'People just weren't doing it, they were trying to cut the crossover type of music. I'd hate to see it get to the point where I couldn't turn on a country radio station and hear some of this traditional music.' The only thing that isn't traditional about Randy is the enormous number of records he sells.

Travis has become a talisman of real country and its limitless potential, if it's sung right and handled with respect. The politely spoken singer has turned conventional marketing wisdom on its head. Emmylou Harris again:

> There have always been, and I'm sure they still exist, record executives who really believe in their hearts that country music doesn't sell, even though it's been around since the thirties. Maybe

41

(*Above*) *George Jones, inspiration for New Country artists like Randy Travis and (opposite centre) Lyle Lovett*

it will never sell the amount of records that rock'n'roll sells, although you've got Randy Travis whose debut album went platinum, and this guy couldn't go pop with a mouthful of firecrackers, as Waylon Jennings would say.

Let's face it, that is a country record. Randy is not like a crossover artist. He's a country artist and he hasn't crossed over, but he's sold a million albums.

In fact, Travis's clean country sound now shifts units fast enough to challenge major rock acts like Bruce Springsteen, and his second album, *Always And Forever*, has sold more than 3 000 000 copies.

The artists lumped together under new country's umbrella (sometimes unwittingly, or even unwillingly) offer glimpses of the entire spectrum of everything that country music has ever been. Country has always been a hybrid form in any case, taking its influences from Africa, England, Ireland, Mexico or Eastern Europe, and that, at least, hasn't changed.

Canadian singer K. D. Lang, often rather tiresomely spelt k. d. lang, has a post-punk haircut, but she hitched up with Patsy Cline's producer Owen Bradley to record her *Shadowland* album. Lang apparently feels that she may even be the reincarnation of Ms Cline, which is either a case of galloping immodesty or a promise of greater things to come. Either way, perhaps she should avoid air travel whenever possible. On the other hand, Ricky Skaggs, whose startling bouffant hair once earned him disqualification from an appearance on *The Old Grey Whistle Test*, is a virtuoso in the old bluegrass music of his native Kentucky. Though he's only in his early thirties, Skaggs has become a new pillar of the old-established *Grand Ole Opry*, which is still broadcast across the Southern states of America on Saturday nights.

As for Skaggs's fellow-Kentuckian Dwight Yoakam (he of the perpetual stetson wedged atop a gleaming crown), his early diatribes against the pollution and corruption of the Nashville industry made him look like a dangerous revolutionary. In fact, Dwight's rantings were only affirmations of his commitment to restoring country's working-class roots and of his particular enthusiasm for Buck Owens and the so-called 'Bakersfield Sound'.

Dwight survived a period in which it looked as though he might be tarred, feathered and run out

(Top) Waylon Jennings – leader of the 'Outlaw' movement and (bottom) Dwight Yoakam, Nashville rebel

of town (particularly after his tirade against CBS, Nashville, when they dropped Johnny Cash from the label a couple of years ago) to become one of Nashville's favourite sons. Both Buck and Bakersfield made a guest appearance on Dwight's 1988 album *Buenas Noches From A Lonely Room*, with Yoakam's cover of Homer Joy's 'Streets of Bakersfield'. They sang it live on network television during the 1988 Grammy awards ceremony too, an event which also featured Randy Travis and rising Texan star Lyle Lovett in a public affirmation of country's new high profile.

'Nashville adopted a "pleasing all of the people all of the time" marketing mentality,' Dwight raged one sunny morning in Los Angeles. 'Well I'm sorry, McDonalds may be able to do that with fast food, but I don't go to McDonalds because it doesn't please me.' Yoakam is a classicist, an extremely well-informed student of country music who insists on a return to the music's virile outspoken roots. His reminders that pioneers of the genre like Hank Williams, Jimmie Rodgers and even the youthful George Jones began their careers as angry young men with a social message are salutary, and too often overlooked.

Maybe we should call artists like Yoakam, Skaggs and Lang 'young country'. But where does that leave Nanci Griffith, clearly identified with the new country camp but a girl who might equally claim to be a folk singer? Or K. T. Oslin, who's fighting a lonely battle for the sexual emancipation of the mature woman? The Judds, the mother and daugher unit whose impeccable harmony singing and 'pure country' sound have won them a shower of awards and accolades since 1984, actually embody two generations every time they step up to the microphone. However, they seem a little less open to change and diversity than some of their contemporaries, and are convinced that thrash metal is a form of torment sent from hell. 'Grandpa, tell me 'bout the good old days,' they chorus plaintively.

If there are any rules, there are far more exceptions. Lyle Lovett displays a breadth of taste and metropolitan sense of irony quite at odds with the enduring image of country's God-fearing, plain language past. The Lord holds no terrors for Lovett. God might forgive his cheatin' lover, he tells us darkly in his song 'God Will', but Lyle

will be damned if he's going to ('and that's the difference between God and me'). If he fits anywhere at all, perhaps it's alongside fellow-Texans Guy Clark and the promising newcomer Darden Smith.

Lovett won't claim to be operating anywhere near 'traditional' country.

> I bought some old Ray Charles records on Atlantic that were done in the fifties, that were great records. I've always liked blues, y'know, in Houston you can hear a lot of blues, so that's really where that came from. The record company hasn't made me feel like 'you'd better stick a fiddle or a steel guitar on there, because this is supposed to be country'.

The labels are learning to leave well alone.

Anyway, the Texans have always come in at a slightly different slant from everyone else, and they tend to have staying power. Joe Ely, from Lubbock, enjoyed brief stardom under the patronage of The Clash at the end of the seventies, then vanished, but has recently returned with two fine albums, particularly *Lord Of The Highway*. There's a sense in which Texans have never really felt that they belonged to the USA. 'Well there's always been that,' Lyle Lovett allows. 'If you're around a Texan for more than a couple of minutes, he'll start to brag about the state.'

Country still sounds good with some rock stirred into it, too. Chris Hillman, one-time bassist with The Byrds but a country player at heart, has been enjoying a new lease of life with his Desert Rose Band, scoring hits like 'I Still Believe In You'. Highway 101 are recognisable by their alternating male/female vocal leads, which may help to account for desriptions of them as a kind of countrified Fleetwood Mac. John Hiatt, enjoying tumultuous critical rehabilitation of late, lives in Nashville but plays with a sizzling Louisiana band, The Goners, and treats country music to the wolfish grin of the born sceptic.

'One more heartfelt steel guitar chord, girl it's gonna do me in,' he sings in 'Memphis In The Meantime', an ode to the greasy good-time soul stew of Tennessee's other Music City. And Texan bruiser Steve Earle has travelled from rockabilly to country-metal over the course of three albums, albeit with somewhat questionable results. He now plays three-hour shows and seems to think he's

Bruce Springsteen, complete with boring anec-
dotes between songs, but let us hope this is just a
phase.

Rosanne Cash, daughter of the legendary Man
in Black, Johnny, is a splendid example of the
futility of applying labels to music. She has established herself at the top of the new Nashville elite
despite being brought up in California and playing
music which owes as much to the country rock of
Buffalo Springfield or The Eagles as it does to her
father's repertoire.

Her recent country hit with her dad's song 'Tennessee Flat-Top Box' perhaps represented a
coming to terms with her own past, but her
albums, like the 1985 *Rhythm & Romance*, have
found her examining personal crises and marital
uproar with courage and great tunes. Her marriage
to songwriter, Rodney Crowell, something of a
force in contemporary Nashville himself, seems to

have been both a challenge and an inspiration to
her.

Her father has no doubts about Rosanne's
musical gifts. 'I think Rosanne will have her day,
getting the award of the year for top country
female vocalist,' Cash rumbled recently. 'I guess
she's what you'd call progressive country, if you
gotta put a brand on it. I think she's the best of
the new breed.'

But Johnny Cash is as confused as anybody else
by the current state of country music.

> I think it's going in about ten different directions,
> I don't know which one is strongest. For a while,
> it had swung back to traditional, with Randy
> Travis and Reba McIntire and George Strait. Even
> Dwight Yoakam sounds like fifties country for the
> most part, though he's a man of the eighties or
> nineties. But there's a new group on the charts
> every week, I don't know what direction country's
> going in.

(Below) Steve Earle

However you modify the term, country is clearly in pluralistic good health. Once something can be neatly tied and labelled, it's probably on the way out. Much of its current vitality doubtless has something to do with the corresponding decline in the potency of rock music, since many of the new country acts might equally have been accommodated under the broad banner of 'rock' in, say, the early seventies.

Rock or pop would habitually give themselves a shot in the arm every now and again by borrowing from some other form of music. (Dylan supposedly played 'folk rock', Malcolm McLaren hit upon opera and African music, The Police adotped reggae and the Beatles were pilfering Indian raga licks twenty years before the current boom in world music.) But it's now country which is routinely absorbing any number of influences. While new hybrids like rap, house and hip-hop steal and sample from other people's recordings with a kind of DIY home-electronics zeal, it's country which is making organic use of a variety of musical forms. Lyle Lovett agrees:

> That's a great observation. About the only place you can hear an Eagles song any more is a country station. It's almost as if country music is broader and more diverse than pop music is. In pop they worry more about the snare sound and stuff.

Country was a crucial ingredient of the first great rock'n'roll revolution of the fifties, and it's become something of a truism of rock history to point to the fusion of southern black music with white hillbilly which gave birth to Elvis Presley's early classics and the great Sun recordings from Sam Phillips' Memphis studio. Buddy Holly, Roy Orbison and the Everly Brothers all had conspicuous country roots too, and many of their biggest hits were recorded in Nashville.

But it's also instructive to trace the line through to rock's great flowering in the sixties and beyond. California's Buffalo Springfield frequently displayed country leanings, and the band's subsequent offshoots included country-rockers Poco, the eclectic Crosby Stills Nash and Young, and Neil Young's various exploits.

Young has been a kind of yardstick for the relative potency of country and rock. In 1985, as new country gathered steam, he released a straight country album called *Old Ways*, toured with country greats like Willie Nelson, and became heavily involved with Farm Aid, when the country community rallied round to raise money for stricken American farmers. 'There's a lot of family heritage that goes back, it's really important, and that's part of country that I can relate to,' Young explained. 'Country looks after its own, unlike rock'n'roll.'

And then there was Gram Parsons, probably the most influential figure in the development of country-rock. His brief stint with the Byrds prompted their fine country album *Sweetheart Of The Rodeo*, he was the motivating force behind the Flying Burrito Brothers, and his solo recordings featuring Emmylou Harris (*G. P.* and *Grievous Angel*) have refused to date. The Parsons influence is audible today, in diluted form, from the likes of Alabama. If it's true to say that Emmylou was a lone standard-bearer for country during the crossover years at the end of the seventies, she gives Parsons much of the credit. 'I was trying to carry on for Gram,' she explained. 'I just sort of took it upon myself to say "OK, how would Gram do it?" It was always a matter of following an emotional instinct, being in the dark but knowing there was something.'

En route, Ms Harris's band became a breeding-ground for musicians who would go on to become influential artists in their own right.

> I was fortunate enough to work with this remarkable group of people who went on to branch out and do other things – Emory Gordy, Ricky Skaggs, Rodney Crowell and Hank DeVito. Steve Fishell, my pedal steel player, produced Rosie Flores, so it just keeps going on.

Emmylou couldn't be more pleased with the way country, 'new' or whatever else you'd call it, is heading.

> It's great to turn on the radio now and hear young kids doing stuff that's as authentic as the music from the fifties, but with real energy and heart and soul, and I think a real dedication. They're putting a rock'n'roll energy and a poetry behind country music, which has always been a tried and true form.

The circle has wobbled a bit from time to time, but it remains unbroken.

ALGERIAN RAI- THE FRENCH CONNECTION

PHILIP SWEENEY

Finding the North African immigrants' *quartier* in Marseilles doesn't take much detective work. For one thing, it's the area hotel receptionists tell you to avoid. For another, it's exactly where newcomers would arrive; a square mile of narrow streets sandwiched between the railway station and the docks. Nicknamed 'the cashbah' by the less welcoming of Marseilles' citizenry, including the city's numerous National Front supporters, it is known more conventionally as the quartier Belsunce. Follow gravity from the forecourt of the splendid *fin de siècle* Gare St Charles and, as you descend the boulevard d'Athenes and plunge off into the warren of steep side roads leading down to the Old Port, the surroundings become more and more Magrebin. Olive-skinned, weather-beaten old men crowd the bars and cafes, drinking tea or beer, smoking and chatting. Veiled women, weighed down with plastic carriers, walk the pavements from halal butcher to fresh mint stall to oriental pâtisserie. The sound of the local Arab language station, Radio Gazelle, drifts out of open windows. At weekends the *quartier* buzzes with commerce as Moroccans, Tunisians and Algerians cross the Mediterranean to visit relations and to shop. Thirty-five thousand visitors are estimated to pass through the area weekly, each spending

(Opposite) Rai's three biggest stars, Cheb Khaled, Chaba Fadela and Cheb Sahraoui with producer Rachid Baba

between £500 and £1000 at its 800 wholesalers and retailers.

Naturally enough, the music business plays its part. Cassette shops offer a huge range of Arab classics and novelties: the great Egyptians Oum Kalthsum and Ferid Al Atrache; Moroccan folk revivalists; the old Algerian poet/singers, the *chioukh*; the endless *sourates* (sung extracts) of the Koran; Berber protest singers of the seventies; and nowadays, in pride of place, Algerian rai music, purveyed by an ever-changing collection of *chebs* (young male singers).

Live music flourishes too. Algerian musicians come over for a few concerts, spend their fee on clothes, electrical appliances or car parts unobtainable at home, and take the ferry back without ever needing to visit Paris, 800 km to the north. After midnight, a range of cafes and clubs begins to fill with a predominantly male clientele. The lower end of the market offers a few beers in the back room of a little bar with a Kabyle vocal and lute duo paid for by a whip-round. For the high rollers there are the cabarets – kitsch arabesque decor, tables around a stage, whisky at £60 a bottle and music perhaps

from a six to eight-piece light classic '*orchestre orientale*', and maybe from time to time a rai singer. During Ramadan the pace quickens as night-time social life intensifies to compensate for the daylight fast.

On a visit in August 1988 I narrowly missed Cheb Khaled, the king of rai, at the Mille et Une Nuits, but struck lucky at the Palmerie, where Cheb Sahraoui and Cheba Fadela were about to start a week of shows. Fadela is a key figure in the world of rai. Her 1979 recording 'Ana M'Hali Enoum' ('I Don't Care About Sleep Anymore'), the first great hit of the new rai, ushered in the decade which has seen the music progress from a marginal niche in its Western Algerian homeland, to a product sought out by international record companies; a chart contender in Europe and a talking point in rock circles around the world. Cliché though it is, the comparison of rai's develop-

ment with that of the blues is apt. Both were types of vulgar street music taken up in more cultured circles for their low-life vitality and transmuted into mass popular entertainment. In the case of rai, the rise to international prominence has been incredibly rapid. Many Algerians are bewildered to learn that a music they still regard as insignificant is attracting media attention halfway around the world.

The roots of the music, and of its name, can be traced back to the port of Oran, in Western Algeria, in the twenties and thirties. The dominant musical form then was the 'chir el melhoun', a rarified and academic sung poetry whose classical Arabic lyrics with their references to deserts, stars and stallions were already irrelevant, even incomprehensible, to the new class of impoverished factory and agricultural workers. The daily reality of the Oran region was hard work in the vineyards and on the great estates, and recreation in the seafront dives. A new music, direct and earthy, evolved as an alternative to melhoun, which continued to be performed by its elderly and respectable guadians, the chioukh (plural of cheikh). Already the refrain 'Ha-er rai!' (roughly meaning 'It's my opinion'), was beginning to be used as an all-purpose adornment and filler, rather like 'Oh yeah' in Anglo-American pop. By the fifties rai, as it had come to be known was largely the preserve of the cheikhates, exclusively female entertainers who animated not only weddings, the traditional occasions for large parties, but also the cafes, brothels and hashish dens of Oran. The cheikhates (of whom the most famous, Cheikha Rimitti El Relizania, is still singing in Paris today) occupied a curiously unstable position, their risqué lyrics tolerated only at a safe remove from polite society, their early recordings widely distributed but subject to police seizure for immorality. In the early seventies President Boumedienne's puritanical clean-up campaign, 'operation anti-drageur', suppressed the cheikhates along with nightclubs and most other manifestations of

(Above) Chaba Fadela and Cheb Sahraoui

decadence and vice.

By this time, however, the musical complexion of the Oran region had diversified. Modern instruments – the violin, trumpet, accordion and guitar – had supplemented or replaced the traditional gasbas (rosewood flute) and guellals (hand-drum). The style known as 'asri' ('Oran modern' or 'folklore Oranais') had grown up with star performers Blaoui El Houari and Ahmed Saber; the latter's mordant and risqué lyrics echoing the tone of the cheikhates. A whole range of external influences had left their mark; 'gnaoui', a black North African percussive style, flamenco and the trumpet *paso dobles* of the bullfight bands from nearby Spain, and Anglo-American pop. In the sixties several electric groups sprung up – The Red Stars, The Drifters, The Vultures – covering Western crazes such as the twist and, in some cases, reviving and modernising favourite numbers from the Oran folklore repertoire.

Prominent among the professional musicians of this period was the trumpeter Messaoud Bellemou, who started his career in the municipal brass band of his home town, Ain Temouchent, and went on to establish himself as a versatile and innovatory bandleader. Bellemou is generally credited with the reinvention of rai as pop rai, and his 1975 recording *Ya Rayi* anticipated the beginning of the current boom by five years.

Around this time Bellemou began working with a young singer/actress, Fadela Zalmat, resulting in the smash hit 'Ana M'Hali Enoum'. This proved to be a perfectly timed *succès de scandale*. The strait-laced years of Boumedienne's clamp-down had loosened just enough to whet the appetite of a youthful but repressed population for sex, drugs and rock'n'roll. Fadela had already outraged conservative opinion with her role as a smoking, drinking, mini-skirted delinquent in the 1976 television film *Djalti*, a sort of Algerian *Blackboard Jungle*. Her new hit gave a burgeoning regional trend national prominence, and opened the floodgates to a deluge of young male rai singers, most of

them prefixing their names with 'Cheb', which means 'young' or 'kid' in pointed contrast to the 'Chioukh' – Cheikh Hamada, Cheikh Al Madani – whose title signified age and respectability.

The chebs were mostly working-class boys who learned their craft at wedding parties, whisky clubs and the cabarets Florida and Biarritz, which continued to be a feature of the Oran seafront. Their songs were about the fast, rebellious lives they aspired to – girls, alcohol, the beach, cars – with a melodramatic undercurrent of the anguish of doomed love and, occasionally, a subdued note of protest at their lack of freedom in a strictly paternalist Islamic state. The strongest lyrics spoke of nights of abandon with forbidden lovers followed by days of agonised self-abasement, drunkenly seeking the unattainable object of their passion. The angst and self-destruction were by no means unrelieved however. Essentially an improvised communal music, most at home in a roomful of dancers, rai was full of asides to the audience, comments, remarks and topical references.

By the eighties, the recorded music market in Algeria, as throughout Africa, was entirely dominated by cassettes, churned out and constantly pirated by dozens of small-time businessmen. A promoter (often the proprietor of a record shop) would pay an artist for the time required to play half a dozen pieces in a two-track 'studio'. With good timing, the last track on a side would come to an abrupt halt just as the tape ran out. A full day in the studio (the morning for rehearsal, the afternoon for recording) would be considered luxurious. To keep the money coming in, artists had to make frequent recordings since the process was both cheap and unremunerative. Although the system was unsophisticated, considerable sales could result. A major hit might sell 150 000 copies, for which a top star like Cheb Khaled would get a one-off fee of between £5000 and £10 000.

In this anarchic world, the brothers Rachid and Ferthi Baba Ahmed rapidly established themselves as the leading creative producers of the new

(Above) Bellemou Messauod – one of the founders of pop rai and (opposite) Cheb Khaled – the King of Rai

wave of pop rai. The son of a well-known player
of the rebab, a traditional single-string violin,
Rachid learned guitar in his teens, toured with the
sixties rock group, Les Vautours (The Vultures),
returned to Arabic pop and by 1980 had his own
eight-track studio in Tlemcen, near Oran, where
he composed and recorded television music. His
was the idea, put into practice first with the singer
Cheb Hamid, of recording an unaccompanied
vocal track and subsequently working at leisure
to construct a backing out of layers of over-dubbed
instruments. By 1988, and the arrival on the scene
of the big Western record companies, Rachid and
Ferthi had opened a new 24-track studio, and had
recorded almost all of the major rai artists.

At this point five rai artists dominated the
scene. Chaba Fadela was still firmly in the top
rank. Fadela had married Mohammed Sahraoui,
a *conservatoire*-trained musician, retired briefly to
produce a baby son and returned triumphantly to
perform in a duo with Sahraoui, a move which
succeeded in attracting a double public; the men
identifying with Sahraoui, the women with
Fadela. Their 1983 recording 'N'Sel Fik' ('You
Are Mine') became one of the greatest successes of
the decade.

In 1986 a rival to Fadela's position as leading
female singer had appeared in the form of Moroc-
can-born Chaba Zahrouania, whose rough, bluesy
voice, trained in the 'meddhates' female orchestras, recalled vividly the raucous and bawdy cheikhates.

The title of king of rai was, and is, incontestably
the property of Cheb Khaled, a talented and char-
ismatic singer and accordion player who rose to
fame by his consistent strong performances, a
string of hits such as 'Hada Raykoum' and 'Sidi
Boumedienne', and a delightfully gossip-worthy,
devil-may-care rock'n'roll lifestyle.

In 1982 a pretender to Khaled's throne emerged
from a television talent contest and over the following three years built a major career with his
high agile voice, shrewd sense of public demand
and polished recordings. The career of the prince
of rai, Cheb Mami, was impeded, if not halted, in
1986 by a two-year spell of national service.

If 1980 marked the start of the pop rai craze, it
was not until the middle of the decade that the
music achieved acceptability on the part of the

Algerian authorities and state-run media. Rai had never been overtly political; the strongest protest element in Algerian music had occurred in the forties and fifties when the bitterness of the burgeoning anti-colonial struggle had coloured the lyrics. However, rai's general concerns – sex and alcohol, and the self as opposed to the state – were anti-establishment, as were the lifestyles of its young devotees. Rai was therefore discouraged, if not exactly persecuted, for a considerable time. As the music infiltrated further into the middle classes and the realisation dawned that rock'n'roll was a safer obsession for the country's youth than Islamic fundamentalism, economic reform or Berber nationalism, the authorities began to support rai, doubtless mindful also of the considerable revenues from sales of cassettes abroad.

In 1983 a relatively innocuous Cheb Khaled song, 'El Mersem' was played for the first time on the radio. In 1985 full-scale festivals were organised in Oran and Algiers. From then on rai concerts began to move out of their traditional locations (private parties and cabarets) and onto the big open-air public stages where audiences of up to 50 000 were possible. The Ryad-el-Feth cultural centre in Algiers, under the directorship of its influential head, Colonel Sonoussi, began to organise massive concerts on the marble forecourt of its huge mall. By 1988 Khaled, Sahraoui and Fadela were still playing the Oran Airport Hotel, the Grand Hotel Tlemcen and the occasional wedding, but were thinking increasingly in the rock-star terms of big concert halls and stadiums.

The continuous back and forth of Algerians to the immigrant communities of Marseilles, Lyon and Paris ensured that the progress of rai was mirrored in its French second home. In January 1986, a festival of rai at Bobigny, a Parisian suburb, featuring all the top chebs, attracted considerable attention from the French media. Increasingly Parisian trend-setters realised that here was an enticingly esoteric new music ripe for discovery. Style magazines had featured for some time a trickle of articles on *le style beur* (*beur* being slang for second-generation Algerian immigrants). Jean-Paul Goude, advertising director and image-creator of Grace Jones, declared himself a fan of Cheb Mami and began to apply the headline-catching visual techniques he had deployed on his

black American 'look' to *le style beur*. Frankfurt, Milan and Tokyo began to pay attention. The rai bandwagon rolled out beyond the threshold of its Algerian stable.

By the end of 1986, the growing prospect of an audience outside the Algerian community had established Paris as an alternative base to Oran or Algiers for a number of rai musicians, though others still did not believe that the international pop market would have anything to do with them. The veteran group Raina Rai were resident in Paris, as was Cheb Mami before his call-up to the army. A number of French promoters were hatching schemes to break various singers in Europe.

For the members of the Parisian rai community the most frequent rendezvous was the Cadran Magenta, a nondescript cafe on the bouelvard Magenta, just down from the great wrought-iron flyover at Metro Barbes-Rochechouart, on the edge of the dilapidated immigrant ghetto district known as the Goutte d'Or. The Goutte d'Or is the commercial hub for the North African immigrant communities of the eighteenth *arondissement* and the big satellite suburbs like Sarcelles and Gennevilliers.

The Cadran Magenta, run by the genial, burly Hafid Ammari, was a meeting-point, a source of reviving expressos and *demis-pression* and a repository of mail and messages for the rai milieu. Prominent among them were the six members of the group Noudjoum el Rai (The Stars of Rai) and two of the singers who regularly perform with them, Cheb Kada and Cheb Dany. Noudjoum el Rai, originally formed in 1980 with a view to playing Western rock in the style of The Rolling Stones and Procul Harum, had switched rapidly to join the rai boom and worked continuously from 1985 backing all the major stars who played in Paris. From their base they waited for a break into something bigger – recording, or perhaps a tour of Europe – and passed the time playing weddings, community association concerts in the suburbs, the occasional Algerian nightclub, and the odd gig at a 'French' club, like the New Morning or Elysee-Montmartre.

Cheb Kada had also done a lengthy spell in the ranks, rubbing shoulders with all the big names. As a child in Oran he had heard the old Cheikh

Hamada and the early rai star Boutelja Belkacen singing in his father's cafe, the Tontonville. His musical career had started at weddings, where he was entrusted with the amplifiers, and where he picked up harmonica and later guitar, slipping into the role of accompanist for a few francs. In 1973 he backed the singer Yasmina on a recording; the accordionist was Cheb Khaled. Diversifying into synthesizer, he became a leading fixture in the clubs in Oran, then in its seventies heyday as the Las Vegas of the Algerian riviera and breeding-ground of the new pop rai. In the Florida, the Biarritz or the Casino de Bouiseville, he would be found animating a dance floor of whisky-fuelled bon-vivants, their pockets stuffed with money and nothing to spend it on. Moving to Paris in 1983, he married a *beurette* and continued in much the same vein.

In early 1987, I accompanied the cheerful, friendly Kada to a typical engagement. It was at a cabaret, La Falaise, just below the Place Pigalle. We arrived at 2am but the small L-shaped room was almost empty until 3.00. The photographer and I sat and drank beer at £9 a glass, looked at the carpeted walls and the twenty red-lit tables, and listened to the backing group – lute, synthesizer, tambourine and derbouka hand-drum – filling in time listlessly. At 3.30, with the room almost full and bottles of whisky and coke enlivening the clientele (70 per cent men aged between thirty and sixty, 30 per cent younger women), Cheb Dany took the stage, raised the microphone to his lips and wailed out the slow sinuous lament 'Amon! Amon!' ('Have pity. Have pity') which is the classic opening to many rai songs. Within minutes, the room was full of dancers, the women with scarves tied around their hips, their arms raised, flamenco style, and thumb and forefinger arched gracefully, doing a neat, reserved, but sexy shimmy. A procession of singers kept the floor crowded for the next few hours and the night ended around 6.30am.

The association of pop rai with the nightclub scene impeded its breakthrough, especially in Algeria, as a suitable entertainment for family concerts and as a broadcastable commodity. As its popularity grew, so a certain toning-down of its more strident vulgarity became evident. Sahraoui and Fadela began to speak of making rai more

polite and professional. Khaled muddled on nonchalantly, remaining enough of a renegade to be interesting and enough of a star to stay in the limelight. The leading proponent of a cleaned up, mass-appeal rai was the ambitious young *prince du rai*, Cheb Mami, who had rapidly perceived the possibilities of a real showbusiness career, and who commented in 1986: 'At the beginning I thought like the other chebs ... I thought I'd come and sing in France to buy a car to take back ... that's rai. Now I'm not thinking of just fun and cars ... I want to make rai known.' Mami was a natural candidate to take the final step that would put rai into the hands of a professional production and distribution network and cash in on the burgeoning European and world interest.

It was not long before Mami found a suitable person to help him achieve this objective. Michel Levy, a former record industry PR man was working for Horizon Music, a small Paris-based record company with an extensive Arab repertoire, which had licensed an LP by Khaled from Algerian producers MCPE and had produced Mami's first European LP. Levy saw that of the two contenders for international stardom, Mami was much the better bet. The unpredictable and irresponsible Khaled was too attached to the rai ethos of quick money and fast living, with no concession to bourgeois taste and a disdain for planning and publicity. Levy became Mami's manager and a succession of neat career moves followed (a new CD recording, a video-cassette for the German market, concerts in America and Japan, the soundtrack music for a Jean-Paul Goude documentary), only to be rudely interrupted by Mami's two-year engagement with the army.

A perfect successor to Mami was ready to fill the gap. Levy already had another young cheb under his wing. Like the prince of rai, he was young, clean-cut, good-looking and ambitious, and Levy now proceeded to guide the new boy into the limelight. Cheb Kader, born Kouider Morabet of Moroccan parents in Oran in 1966, had moved with his family first to Mulhouse and then to Paris, where he played with a succession of amateur groups either in the style of the Moroccan seventies stars Nass El Ghiwane or the newer Casablancan music *bidaoui*. In 1986 he joined Horizon

(Opposite background) Cheb Khaled and (opposite top) Cheb Kada

Music as a delivery boy and succeeded in persuading the company to distribute a privately recorded disc, which had cost him £300 to cut. In December of that year he replaced the absent Mami on the bill of an SOS Racisme concert and has never looked back. The following two years brought top-ten hits in Germany and Switzerland, considerable television exposure in France, including a starring role in the first rai drama, and concerts in a dozen other countries. All this established him as one of the leading rai artists everywhere except Algeria, where he remains virtually unknown.

Fears that the rai scene would suffer from the new commercial orientation and follow other once-vital musical forms towards vapid disco gloss have proved unfounded. On the contrary, a refreshing variety of styles seems to be flourishing. Cheb Khaled produced a slick and expensive LP with the jazz/rock arranger Safy Boutella, backed by a reputed £85 000 of Algerian government money, but the result was a critical and commercial flop, above all in Algeria where it was judged 'not real rai'. Khaled, who never bothered to promote his expensive white elephant anyway, continued artistically undiminished. A new lease of life among the rai precursors manifested itself, with Messaoud Bellemou leading a return to fashion of the silvery quarter-tone trumpets and rough, exciting percussion he had pioneered. Cheikha Djenia, Fadela's former employer, took on the chebs at their own game by recording a pop rai cassette with the up and coming Cheb Abdelhak. New artists – Cheb Hasni, Cheb Tahar, Chaba Zahouania – fill the Biarritz and other Oran cabarets vacated by the upwardly mobile Sahraoui and Fadela, while Cheb Mami recently completed his national service and returned to the fray. Rai's ability to harness the distinctive Arabic voices of the various chebs and chabas with a highly sophisticated modern pop sound lies at the heart of its appeal – an appeal that in the short space of a decade has taken it out of the clubs and bars of Oran and put it on the international stage.

WORLD MUSIC MINING-
THE INTERNATIONAL TRADE IN NEW MUSIC
RICK GLANVILL

I received a phone call in the spring of 1989, from a representative of a top-forty British band. Their new LP, he informed me, resounded with distinct African undertones. They'd done their homework, buying up some of the increasingly available and startlingly fine recordings currently being made by African musicians in Paris. 'But what we need,' he ventured, 'is an authentic African voice to sing gibberish – at least to our ears – over the top of some tracks.'

A sign of the times. The late eighties will be remembered as the era when 'world music' became marketable and 'world musicians' came face to face with the cutting edge of the international recording industry.

Considering it began life purely as a means to gain extra exposure for non-mainstream sounds, the term 'world music' has had a remarkably successful two-year life. In 1987, eleven independent record labels, specialists in licensing or recording artists from 'untapped' sources such as Africa, Asia, South America and the Caribbean, first named this media babe. From its conception as a customer-friendly category that would look sharp on record shop 'browser boards', 'world music' has grown into a business buzzword, championed by the European and American media.

Hannibal

EWV 6 A

MAHLATHINI and the MAHOTELLA QUEENS

THOKOZILE

Side 1.
1. THOKOZILE. (4.11)
COMPOSER: S. M. NKABINDE/WEST NKOSI
2. LILIZELA MLILIZELI. (4.13)
COMPOSER: MARKS MANKWANE
3. SIBUYILE. (3.07)
COMPOSER: MARKS MANKWANE
4. NINA MAJUBA. (4.24)
COMPOSER: S. M. NKABINDE/WEST NKOSI

All titles published by Mavuthela Music
Produced by West Nkosi

Style

Sterns
AFRICA

Side X
33⅓ RPM
Stereo

STERNS 1033
© 1988 STERN'S MUSIC
© 1988 STERN'S AFRICA

LE POUVOIR D'UN COEUR PUR
1. Mane mi foul
2. Deresma (5'10")
3. Tayo Bara (6'20")
THIONE SECK

Western pop is currently undergoing a recession of creativity. At international record company forums like Midem or the New Music Seminar, the talk is of the dearth of fresh talent in Britain and America. The 'world music' stands are the only ones staffed by enthusiastic and knowledgeable people. Executives listen to descriptions of the size of markets in Brazil and Nigeria; of the hordes of prodigious artists waiting to be 'discovered'. They become interested when they hear of the enormously lucrative trade of 'world beat' to Japanese consumers.

For decades, the music multinationals like Polygram and EMI have presided contentedly over monopolies in the Third World, content to export rock and pop to their Lagos, Rio or Johannesburg subsidiaries, and harness local talent solely for the domestic (often massive) market. The surge of interest in 'world music' has made these sleeping giants wake up to the global potential of artists for so long kept under wraps. With little extra commitment of resources, the majors are rushing to promote global pop, the only fresh thing on their musical menu.

Some of the larger companies have tried before. Island Records, with its ears-open reputation, blazed a trail into the Latin barrios of New York in the seventies. They released two compilations of salsa music which were then poorly received but are now much sought after.

Island Records were first on the scene again with Nigerian music, signing one of the country's great juju stars, King Sunny Ade in 1983. After the debut success of the LP *Synchro System*, *Aura* surprisingly bombed a year later. Ade was dropped, but the label has maintained a commitment to licensing records and signing acts from Africa, South America and the Caribbean. They currently have Salif Keita, Ray Lema and Los Van Van on their Mango subsidiary.

Virgin Records also entered the fray in the early eighties, trying their luck with Ade's great juju rival Chief Ebenezer Obey for a brief, unsuccessful period. Virgin now handle Youssou N'Dour, Sipho Mabuse and Nusrat Fateh Ali Khan's material, partially overseen by British rock singer and 'world music' enthusiast Peter Gabriel.

The eighties have also seen the growth of the smaller independent labels. Some are owned and run by musicians themselves, as part of a self-contained and carefully monitored trading organisation, properly representing the artists' interests. Such companies are rare, and confined to major artists like Tabu Ley or his great Zairean rival Franco.

Other companies were established by those wishing to license and press music from overseas. After some success, the company might expand to distribute themselves. Stern's, a record store in London, and Melodie in Paris have earned worldwide reputations in doing so, not least in Africa. In London, the Earthworks company of Jumbo and Mary Vanrenen emerged in the eighties as a pioneer in the independents' approach of seeking out the best from abroad and licensing the repackaged product for the increasingly attentive British public. Earthworks' successes with the two southern African compilations *Viva Zimbabwe!* and *Indestructible Beat Of Soweto* surprised many of the major labels and helped open up the British scene.

Stern's decision to go one step further and record original material led to great success with Malian singer Salif Keita. Following his seminal hi-tech LP *Soro* in 1987, Keita was snapped up by Island/Mango. Globestyle, the global pop arm of Ace Records in London, took a chance on a singer little known outside of her native Israel, Ofra Haza, and had a chart hit with her before Warner Brothers signed her up.

In the rush to license and record the wealth of talent emerging from the developing world, there is plenty of evidence to suggest that musicians are leaving themselves open to mistreatment and financial exploitation. Africans, frequently too naive or trusting to question the ways of the music business in the West, seem to be particularly vulnerable. Three examples illustrate the point.

One Zimbabwean band toured Britain for two months in 1987, frequently doing two performances a day. They were paid £7 per diem, out of which they were required to buy food. The booking fee due to them at each gig was insubstantial for a seven-piece group on the road. One night, when the tour organisers revealed they had forgotten to arrange accommodation, the band had to sleep in a railway station. Amazingly, they were still happy to work with the same promoter

(Opposite) Nigeria's King Sunny Ade who once suffered an ignominious walkout by his band

a year later, but were refused a booking on the grounds that they owed him money from the previous dates!

Unworldliness can have more serious long-term effects, especially in the area of contracts. There is one in existence between a West African kora player and a London management company which gives the company sole rights to fourteen songs. Neither duration of contract nor money are mentioned. In this particular case, fourteen songs is the equivalent of four albums. Legally, the agreement may not even be worth the paper it is written on. It is the principle which causes concern.

Eleven-year-old kora player Pa Jobarteh toured Britain last year for several weeks, for the most part chaperoned by a professional English childminder. No member of his family was brought over from the Gambia and he only had brief contact with anyone he could talk to in anything but English (which fortunately he speaks pretty well). He was regularly booked to appear last on bills around the country – often performing as late as 1am. One such occasion was on the night before the Womad festival in St Austell. As soon as he finished playing, he was driven through the night to the Cornish concert site, where he took the stage the same day, some fourteen hours later. One friend of the family, concerned at Jobarteh's treatment, and wary of the booking agency's motives, described it as 'a freak show'.

Such stories can be added to the well-documented litany of exploitation and abuse associated with the popular music industry. Nowadays, Western pop acts surround themselves with a plethora of legal and financial advisers, but world musicians often suffer from their inexperience and their transient currency in the Western music scene. They visit Europe for maybe a few months; they sign to labels that maintain only long-distance contact; and they are willing to accept unsatisfactory conditions for a pitch at the European and North American market. Moreover, their cultural background does not prepare them for the wheeler-dealing that is a necessary aspect of recording and performing in the West.

At the risk of over-simplifying the nature of the relationship between the West and 'world musicians', it is too often reminiscent of colonial trade patterns. In a very real sense, the music of South

(Opposite) Fela Kuti – scourge of Decca, Nigeria

America, Africa and Asia is being mined as a raw resource. Under the monopolies the major labels enjoy, many important decisions – what to release and where, for instance – are made by the parent company. Locally-recorded albums are pressed and packaged abroad, then exported back as the 'refined' product in much the same way as the Gambia, a major exporter of groundnuts, imports tubs of peanut butter.

Some 'world musicians' have become adept at dealing with the intricacies and iniquities of the relationship. Ruben Blades, Salif Keita, Mory Kante and West Nkosi are expert in signing deals and getting what they want. Artists like these are still in a minority and, surprisingly perhaps, exploitation by outsiders has not encouraged solidarity between the musicians themselves. In many bands, the leader not only holds the purse strings, but owns all the instruments. It is common for band leaders to take 50 per cent of door money at a gig, sharing the remainder amongst the rest – maybe as many as thirty musicians – according to their individual experience. Revolts over pay and conditions are not unheard of. King Sunny Ade suffered the indignity of a mass walkout by his band in Japan some years back.

The lack of solidarity between musicians in the developing world is part of a music business infrastructure that for many years has been loaded against the musician. In many places, royalties on records sales are not paid to, and indeed not expected by, musicians. Subsidiaries of major Western labels conveniently choose to adopt local business practices. Afrobeat inventor Fela Kuti took exception to this and, with some of his twenty-seven wives, once occupied the offices of Decca Nigeria for a fortnight to protest about non-payment of royalties. Two of the controversial star's wives had babies in situ before Decca relented.

The worst offenders, though, are the independent mainland labels. Musicians are paid a cash fee – or its equivalent in kind – and may

perhaps expect something later from the producer or label boss if the record sells well. Ethiopian singer Aster Aweke's experience is by no means unique. She was given a sound system by the financiers of one of her recordings. The album became a massive hit, for which she received no further financial reward. Her 'gift' was also a useful promotional aid.

As with everything there are exceptions. Record producer Ibrahima Sylla has adapted his operation to make sure that his artists also benefit. Sylla is a black African working simultaneously within the European and African markets, and knows their intricacies like no other. He has recorded, amongst others, Salif Keita (the *Soro* LP), Sam Mangwana (*Aladji*) and Kasse Mady (*Fode*).

Sylla carries with him huge wads of cash, with which to cross the palms of his regular musicians or protégés. Unlike many in his position, Sylla spends money on his production, and ploughs profits back into future projects. He is a progressive sound maker, drawing together musicians and arrangers with different skills, energetically promoting his music and defeating tape pirates back home by releasing and distributing his music in bulk to every market. His operation, with its interest in developing artists, attention to quality and understanding of local needs, provides a sharp contrast with some multinationals. But Sylla is no angel. He is not above signing artists to contracts, the full implications of which they may not understand. Sylla had Kasse Mady sign a five-year contract when he took him under his wing. Mady signed, even though he cannot read and may not have been fully aware of the contract's contents.

Producers, who dominate the world beat scene, can be regarded perhaps as a necessary evil. Kassav, the most successful band the French Caribbean has ever produced, are now signed internationally to CBS/Epic. Before that, they worked with Henri Debs, who, along with brother and rival George, has the Antilles recording industry sewn up. Kassav's Jocelyn Beroard remembers

(Above) Salif Keita and (opposite) Papa Wemba, King of the Sapeurs

how 'we always had to fight for our money. But then again, Debs helped us to get where we are now by his recordings and promotion.' It might have been different. The Debs brothers have been known to sit on recordings, only releasing them when they deem the time to be right.

Most musicians are aware that breaking into markets to whom the name, let alone the sound of their music is alien, requires compromise. The position of the producer is a powerful one. He can be the bridge from one market to another; a cultural interpreter or a destructive influence. British pop engineer Martyn Young conjured a hellish vision of Afro-house music from Mory Kante's top forty single 'Ye Ke Ye Ke', complete with 'acid' synth work and a total abnegation of the traditional elements – kora-harp, Kante's vocals – which listeners found attractive.

Martin Meissonnier took his production skills to King Sunny Ade's *Aura* LP, and stripped it down to jarring beat-box rhythms in preference to the swaying complexities of Nigerian percussion. More recently and successfully, he has produced Zairean singer Papa Wemba, blending soukous with the Western production values Wemba readily accepts – he is after all on the verge of a breakthrough in Europe. Says Wemba:

> You have to come to Europe to record, because Africa doesn't have the studios, the producers or the promoters. When you use a European producer, it's only natural that you will have European influences. And anyway, the music must progress; back home they play the same sound they did when I left in the seventies.

For many artists, moving to Europe remains a statement of intent and professional ambition. Markets are potentially larger, technology is available and a huge American audience is one step away. Success, however, is not guaranteed. Some eke out a tiny living doing sessions for as little as £5 per night. Ringo Star (not the Beatle, the Paris-based Zairean guitarist) has played in London for just such a fee. He'd do it again too – London is still considered *la capitale de rock*; the place to play. Nevertheless, (as described in Chapter 1), Paris has an infrastructure in which Africans participate fully, unlike London. It also boasts the most exciting African music – the two things might well be related.

Most of the great music that reaches us via Paris has its roots in former French colonies like Senegal and Zaire. Despite the extraordinary creativity of a country like Nigeria, Anglophone countries have failed to match this prodigious, high-quality output. What separates Anglophone countries from the rest of the continent is the influence foreign record companies have over the local music scenes. An example is Britain's Serengeti Records.

Run by Mike Wells and Mike Andrews, whose brother Ron heads Polygram Kenya, Serengeti operates throughout Africa – Kenya, Zambia, Zimbabwe, South Africa, Nigeria and the Ivory Coast – and in other parts of the world like Barbados, Brazil and India. Wells has a large international set-up, with connections built up over his years working worldwide for EMI.

All labels, major or independent, which have an interest in licensing African music know Mike Wells. New companies interested in licensing music from the regions Serengeti covers may be surprised when they are put in touch with this Home Counties businessman in his fifties. But Wells is the middle-man for Anglophone territories the world over. He even sells reggae and soca

to Africa and Asia, and Hindi music to Asian expatriates around the globe.

To sapling companies, Serengeti represents a Santa's grotto of goodies. Mike Wells will deliver hundreds of cassettes to your door. Select the tracks you like, and another compilation from South Africa, Zimbabwe or Zambia finds its way into the record racks.

Many great recordings have seen the light of day in Britain solely because of Wells' efforts. Salif Keita's *Soro*, is one, and Ladysmith Black Mambazo's *Induku Zethu* is another. The list of 'discoveries' also includes Ivory Coast reggae star Alpha Blondy and myriad other artists featured on Kenyan and other compilations. The Serengeti network does, however, have drawbacks, such as the mark-up the company places on its goods. Acting as it does as a middle-man, it charges a percentage of the wholesale price for each record

and cassette (of which Serengeti retains a third and the label of origin takes the rest). This can represent a considerable slice from a small label's profit margin, and may discourage investment in developing the artists concerned.

And, given that communications between licensor and licensee can be somewhat erratic, artists do not always know in advance of their music's release abroad. It is a sobering experience to be with a musician in one of London's record shops when they first see their name on a smartly designed sleeve.

However, if more European companies start to deal directly with their counterparts abroad, and encourage them to take a more active role in the promotion of their best talent, things will improve. There is clearly a need, too, for artists to be kept better informed as to when and where their music is being licensed.

Respect is something many world musicians

have yet to be given in several quarters. The major labels seem to have trouble pronouncing names or remembering if an artist is on their roster. Yet the well-meaning enthusiast can do similar damage. A professed love of music is not enough.

In recent years, the gap between the public purity of small-scale operations involved in 'world music', and the private reality has widened. Early pioneers in the field might feel aggrieved that others have jumped on the bandwagon and – more irritatingly – made money where they have not. But there is criticism of those who are now 'cashing in their chips', while drawing on their image as keepers of the world music flame and using their influence and contacts to take the financial slice they consider their due. And why should the major labels (with their established system of royalty rates, advances and resources to support touring bands) be seen as wicked, while the independents (starved of resources, cutting corners and offering stripped-to-the-marrow deals) are viewed as the goodies? There's an old saying: nice don't pay the rent.

The innocence of small companies in the West has long since evaporated in the face of the 'world music' explosion. Nowadays, 'world music' promoters, large and small, demand film and recording rights, and all their lucrative spin-offs, with ruthless tenacity.

Major or independent, all record companies now dance to the same tune, and it is one that world musicians must learn fast. To some extent the musicians themselves are to blame. Anxious for success outside their homelands, too ready to accept terms they should dismiss, and too willing to trust the counsel of Europeans with a vested interest, they not only offer themselves for the slaughter, but set dangerous precedents which others will have to follow.

It is time the musicians showed some unity, fought for what is justly theirs, and took control in the way that Western artists are learning to do. 'World music' would be all the richer for it.

THE MUSIC OF WEST AFRICA

A PERIOD OF TRANSITION

JENNY CATHCART

From Gorée Island off the coast at Dakar, Senegal, millions of slaves took their last look at Africa. Those who arrived in the Americas had nothing but their determination to survive and to retain their identity. They were comforted by their own songs and dances which were to make a unique contribution to American popular music. The roots of blues, soul, jazz and gospel music go back to those immigrants who were forced to make their homes in the New World.

Today's African pop musicians are replying with a new cultural synthesis of traditional African music and Western pop styles. Collaborations between Western and African musicians are cutting across musical frontiers, breaking down cultural barriers, and making a major contribution to what is now termed 'world music'.

Since the twelfth and thirteenth centuries, West Africa has had one of the richest seams of musical activity in the world, developed by a system of patronage common to all courtly traditions. The kings of the Ghana and Mandinka Empires had 'griots' who combined the functions of spokesmen for the people, chief advisers to the kings, and court entertainers. The king never spoke directly to the people but sent his griot into the village square to beat his drum and deliver his message

(Opposite) Salif Keita, descendant of Sundiata Keita, most famous of the Manding kings

or proclamation. The griot was renowned for his common sense, so when the king needed guidance, it was the griot who recalled ancient solutions to current problems. There were also griots who had an unfailing talent for finding the *mot juste* and the sweetest melody to praise the king and his nobles. Moreover, the griot family castes liked to keep their secrets, and the Kouyates, the Diabates, the Secks or the Niangs have intermarried for generations in order to guard their own mysterious gifts.

In the modern world of mass communications, with music readily available from one nation to another via radio, television and satellite, griots can no longer resist the pressures to broadcast their talents. The moment has arrived when they can share what they know with the rest of the world and be influenced in their turn by the music of other cultures. A significant number of West African musicians, whose work is rooted in these ancient traditions, are now achieving international recognition. Youssou N'Dour, the most popular singer in Senegal, is a direct descendant of the griots through his mother's Mboup family who belong to the praise-singing side of the tradition. Then there are the Diabates – Toumani Diabate the young virtuoso kora player, and the singer Kasse Mady Diabate, both from Mali; and Sekou and Sona Diabate from Guinea. Sekou Diabate Bembeya plays with the group Bembeya Jazz and his sister, Sona, with the all female band Les Amazones.

There are West African musicians of enormous talent who do not necessarily belong to the tightly knit griot community but who are also contributing to this process of musical cross-fertilisation. Ali Farka Toure belongs to the Toure family who have the reputation of being marabouts or holy men in the African Islamic tradition. With his brand of African blues, he can communicate with any audience in the West. Baaba Maal played guitar and sang with the Senegalese National Troupe until he formed his electric band Dande Lenol in 1983. Dande Lenol (Voice of the Race), play a form of African reggae which they call yela. It is a style which has proved immensely popular with audiences in Paris and London. Salif Keita is a direct descendant of Sundiata Keita, the most famous of the Manding kings. He is

extremely proud of his noble birth but felt that he was destined to become a singer, filling the role traditionally taken by those whom generations of Keitas paid to sing their praises. His music has been acclaimed as the perfect fusion of traditional and modern, of African and Western musical styles. He and the others have now become *ambassadeurs* for African music in general and West African music in particular. 'Modern pop music is like a tree,' says Keita. 'The leaves and branches are reggae, soul and funk. The trunk is jazz and the roots are African music.'

Ali Farka Toure lives on a farm in Niafunke on the banks of the Niger up river from Mopti. He began by playing the djurkel, a one-string guitar made from a small calabash. The skin is taken from a cow's head and the hair from a horse's tail. He soon discovered he had a natural gift. 'I take the little guitar and when I play, the music comes from the Jinns, the Spirits.' He has transposed the same technique to the modern acoustic and electric guitar and his style of playing and singing is uncannily reminiscent of the blues. He has been compared to legendary American bluesmen like Muddy Waters and John Lee Hooker, both of whom he admires. In fact the first time he heard the music of John Lee Hooker he thought that he must be from Mali.

There is someone playing the music of my country but he doesn't know it. Before that, I had heard Albert King, Jimmy Smith, Ray Charles, James Brown. I listened to those people but I swore they were Malian. People talk to me about the blues but I say I will play you the jaba, the tangani, the hekam, so why don't you call it that?

Similarly, the rhythm that underpins Baaba Maal's yela is easily recognisable as reggae but is in fact a modernised form of the music the female griottes have always sung.

From daybreak till nightfall, whatever their chores, the women sang and composed songs. As they pounded the grain in the middle of the compound, the musicians sat around accompanying them. If you listen to the women of the Bhundu in southern Senegal as they sing and dance their yela, you will notice that the way they clap their hands resembles the beat of the rhythm guitar when we play it, and the alternating drum beat represents their accompaniment played on a

(Background) Bembeya Jazz with Sekou Diabate on the right

(Top) Baaba Maal and (bottom) Toumani Diabate, from the renowned griot family the Diabates

simple kitchen calabash. When Africans are modernising their music, they bring out what is in their own traditions, and there are definite similarities between that music and the music of black people in Jamaica or America.

Baaba Maal now lives in Dakar, the capital of Senegal, but remains nostalgic for village life, for the Africa of his childhood in the Fouta – the northern region which borders the Senegal river; a more 'authentic' Africa, less influenced by the outside world than Dakar. When he sings 'Bayo' ('The Orphan') one feels the intensity of that call to his homeland.

> If God could turn me into a pigeon
> Like that golden pigeon we call Mariama
> I could fly off and land at Douwayra
> Back home where my folks are.
>
> If God could give me everything I wish for,
> A long life, happiness and prosperity,
> Then I would live always beside
> Those who are dear to me
> My parents and my friends.

Baaba Maal's parents are both dead but it was his mother who did most to encourage him in his music, sitting with him during guitar lessons and teaching him the classical court dances that are now such an important part of his style. She inspires him even today and he frequently calls her name 'Aida' in his songs. This sense of family loyalty is just one aspect of Baaba Maal's respect for the ancient traditions of his homeland. The Toucouleur people of the Fouta region are renowned for their piety and Baaba Maal's full name is El Hadj Baaba Maal – a 'Hadji' being the name given to one who has made the pilgrimage to Mecca. He has the air of an elegant aesthete, the mystic tendencies of a Sufi. Among his own people he is known for his strong character and deep intelligence. In Dakar, they like to call him 'Baaba Bien' and refer to him as the intellectual among the local musicians.

Like singers in the griot tradition, Baaba Maal's songs often have a moral and a message. In Africa, they say that what comes from the heart goes to the heart. Baaba Maal feels that musicians can touch people's feelings and thoughts more directly than any politician and his sense of tradition has

not prevented him from using this power. Many of his songs express a commitment to progressive ideas for social and political change. The late President Sankara of Burkina Faso, who shared many of Baaba Maal's views on cultural revival and women's emancipation, was an admirer. Sankara, a musician himself, used to play Baaba Maal's song 'Demgalam' ('My Language') each morning. Being Peul, he was proud of an artist who sang in Poular, the language which is common to the Toucouleur and Peul people.

Ironically, it was this same song which created problems for Baaba Maal in Mauritania where the regime has been accused of discriminating against the darker-skinned, casted people who are mainly from the Fouta region. The Fouta was divided at Independence in 1960 by a redrawn border between Mauritania and Senegal. In one dramatic move, the Mauritanian police smashed all the Baaba Maal cassettes in the capital Nouakchott. Baaba Maal has sworn not to go back to Mauritania until all political prisoners are released. He thinks especially of several of his own school friends who are being held captive in appalling conditions.

This willingness to criticise is extended to the outmoded customs and traditions which govern the casted society into which he was born. The song 'Wango' refers to a marriage rendered impossible by a rigid caste system, while 'Dental' calls for unity and tolerance. Baaba Maal believes that West African musicians (who have long been considered an inferior class) gained a new standing as communicators when he joined Youssou N'Dour, Thione Seck, Super Diamono and other Senegalese artists at a concert organised by the charity UNICEF in Dakar in 1986. There have been others, notably Africa Santé, a concert in aid of health programmes in Africa, and one in support of SOS Racisme, the anti-racist organisation which has its headquarters in Paris and is dedicated to helping the immigrant community.

In 1988, when Youssou N'Dour set off on the Human Rights Now! tour (with Peter Gabriel, Bruce Springsteen, Sting and Tracy Chapman) to inform people around the world about the Universal Declaration of Human Rights, he was taking the next step in the modernisation of the ancient griot tradition.

RHYTHMS OF THE WORLD

Some of the concerts were like other pop concerts but in certain places, the audience reaction was such that it felt as if we were messengers who had been sent to the planet to make things known that people up to now had been unaware of.

N'Dour's achievement at home in Senegal had already been remarkable. He began his career at a time when his country was anxious to revive its own Wolof culture which had been submerged by years of French colonisation. The trend to modernise traditional Senegalese music had already begun but N'Dour came with a determination to advance the process. He called his music 'mbalax', a Wolof word which describes the distinctive percussive rhythm that lies at its heart. He realised that traditional rhythmic elements could be transferred to guitars and synthesisers in a way which offered endless potential for experimentation and development without diluting the power of the original sound.

Jo Ouakam, artist and leading authority on West African music and culture, is unequivocal about N'Dour's contribution:

Youssou is an innovator who has always surprised us and will continue to surprise us. He is capable now of working with any musician on any planet. That deep emotion, that sensitivity, that simplicity, that humanity, that pragmatism which is never arrogant can only come from an exceptional being, a person with what we call genius.

In 1958, musicians, mostly from Anglophone countries such as Ghana and Nigeria, began arriving in Dakar, drawn by the cosmopolitan atmosphere and the French bias towards things cultural. They had English names like Johnson and Harrison, and they played wind instruments rather than percussion. Zaireans came too, believing that Dakar would be the first step towards the *métropole*, Paris. The World Festival of Negro Arts held in Dakar in 1966 drew attention to President Senghor's own ideas about negritude, and brought inspiration to Western artists like Picasso and Braque who were interested in African carving. It also highlighted the negro contribution to world music through negro spirituals and jazz.

Towards the end of the sixties, the band leaders gradually left Dakar, some to go to Europe, and some to the Ivory Coast which was beginning to replace Senegal as the centre of attraction for West African musicians. Then Senegalese, notably the saxophonist Papa Samba Diop, Ibra Kasse and Cheikh Tidiane Tall, filled the vacuum with Afro-Cuban sounds that suited the dancers in the Miami Club, the Sahel or the Moulin Rouge. Slowly, traditional African drums began to enter the scene, some from the southern region of Casamance with a Djola band called The Watusita, and some from the Wolof tradition with the groups Baoab and The Star Band. Wolofisation really began when singers decided to sing in their own language rather than in French or Spanish. The stage was set for the young man who put the definitive seal on Senegalese popular music. Jo Ouakam believes that

Youssou N'Dour imposed his extraordinary voice, singing local variations in the manner of his griot parents, but he seemed to renew his inspiration every five years, making gigantic efforts to advance his music beyond the borders of Wolof culture and out into the international scene.

Today, a Youssou N'Dour concert in Dakar resembles any pop concert in the West, with crowds queueing to fill the stadium, ambulances waiting in the wings to carry off fainting members of the audience, and, at the end, a final stampede to get a glimpse of the man himself as he makes a quick getaway. Those who are lucky enough to spot him shout out the current slogan 'Hey you! An Ami?' which is the Wolof chorus from a recent song, 'Hey Youssou, where is Ami (nata)?'

Alongside his phenomenal live success, N'Dour's recorded output in Africa has been extraordinary. With his group Super Etoile De Dakar, he has produced fourteen cassettes and several albums including the classic *Immigrés* which introduced his work to Western audiences. His new record, *The Lion*, recorded in Dakar and Paris with all the back-up of a major record label, is arguably the most innovative crossover album to date. Its producer, Georges Acogny is also Senegalese. He began his career as a jazz musician but is now one of the new wave of pop producers based in England.

What I feel is that this record is going to break a few barriers that have always been there, that is between jazz, pop, rock, soul and African music – all these elements are on the same album. I

(Opposite centre) Youssou N'Dour

74

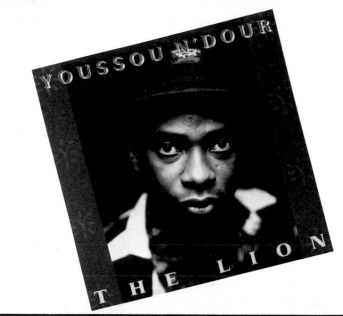

remember back in Senegal going to a club to see Youssou play. Senegalese people were going crazy over his music and I was hoping that one day the rest of the world might have the same reaction — and that day has come.

In keeping with the griot tradition, there has always been a good deal of social comment in N'Dour's songs. His subjects range from life in Dakar to Nelson Mandela and African history. On *The Lion* his writing remains true to this tradition but also reflects the huge variety of musical and cultural influences he has been exposed to in the last two years. 'Shakin' The Tree', co-written with his friend and collaborator Peter Gabriel, pinpoints the current desire amongst the women in Senegal for liberation. The chorus, which is structured like a Western pop song, is sung in English and is a phonetic rendering of the original Wolof. In 'Old Tuscon' N'Dour takes a quintessentially American theme and subjects it to a thoroughly African treatment. The title track to the album 'The Lion' boasts a chorus that immediately evokes the feel and tone of a classic sixties pop song.

Salif Keita's album *Soro* with its highly sophisticated 48-track digital sound has been equally instrumental in transforming and popularising the traditional music of West Africa. Produced in Paris by another Senegalese, Ibrahima Sylla, *Soro* has set an impressive target for African artists in terms of record sales. Released over eighteen months ago, *Soro* has approached the 40 000 mark, compared to the 5000 copies usually sold in the West by African musicians. This success looks as if it will only be matched by *The Lion* or Keita's new record *Ko-Yan*.

Keita has lived in Paris since the early eighties because that seems to him the best way to record and promote his music outside Mali. However, he regularly returns to his native village, Djoliba, some 40 km from Bamako, to renew his inspiration and cleanse himself of modern city life.

I am very happy to have been born here in the depth and the sweetness of what is natural. I went elsewhere and I saw scientific life and I saw other societies and I saw that I was born where I should have been.

Keita was born an albino and Sina, his father, says he was so white that people wondered if he was really a human being. Some even thought that he must be an angel but he was certainly not treated as one by his own people. Children just three or four years old used to spit at him in the streets and he was reduced to living with the down-and-outs in the market area of Bamako after the local teacher training school rejected him because of his poor eyesight. Keita has always felt himself to be an outsider, acutely aware of his abnormality. 'I am different which is not my fault nor that of those around me but I was discontented and I blamed people. In order to pardon myself I learnt to meditate.' His own definition of himself is the 'cursed prophet'; cursed because his father, who had been told that those who become too involved in Islam would not live long, sent him to the French school in the village instead of the Koranic school. Keita has always been drawn to the Muslim faith — one of the striking features of his music is the hypnotic power of his wailing Islamic singing. And he is cursed too perhaps because he embodies a contradiction — he was born with white skin but is black — and because he has rejected the role society expected of him — he is a singer when he should have become an aristocratic landowner like his father. 'I think I will finally purify myself. I am trying now to do that, to find God again, to make up for my mistakes, to work for God's cause. Maybe one day I will no longer be cursed . . .'

Keita justifies his chosen profession as a singer by stressing its noble didactic function. In a way, he is now the teacher he always wanted to be. His texts bring a message for peace and harmony in society and are fundamentally religious. 'I think that all musicians, all artists, are in some measure prophets. Art comes from the heart and the heart is nearer to God.'

His unique vocal style is the result of years of

(Background) Percussion instruments from West Africa and (opposite bottom) Ali Farka Toure —
Africa meets the blues

training and practice. He started by using his voice to chase monkeys from the fields around his father's farm. He went on to play guitar in the bars and restaurants of Bamako and continued to sing with the Rail Band at the Buffet de la Gare and later with Les Ambassadeurs at the Motel de Bamako. Les Ambassadeurs were so named because they had musicians from almost every country in West Africa. They played music that included interpretations of popular dance music from Cuba to Russia. They sang the songs of Otis Redding, James Brown, Charles Aznavour and many others. In 1978, Les Ambassadeurs went to Abidjan and recorded 'Mandjou', a song which immortalised them in Africa and made Keita internationally famous.

With the release of *Ko-Yan*, Keita looks set to consolidate his position at the centre of the world music stage. He is aware that this is an era of exchange and that it is not just Western artists and audiences who are widening their musical horizons. Keita believes that in order to develop, musicians from West Africa must recognise that it is also a period of transition and learn to 'mix what is useful with what is good'. Out of this musical cross-breeding will come the African music of the future. 'The traditions which we don't need in Africa will disappear because there will be a fusion between our profound culture, our powers, our spiritual possibilities and those of the rest of the world.'

HUNGARY AND BULGARIA- A LIVING TRADITION

JOE BOYD

Hungary

The twentieth century has seen a veritable tide of Afro-American music sweeping the musical traditions of Europe before it. All popular rhythms now derive in some measure from the 'dark continent'. Morris dance, yodelling, The Norwegian eight-stringed fiddle, the polka, all are receding rapidly into the history books. Yet suddenly in the late eighties Bulgarian and Hungarian music have begun to reach the same world music audiences who flock to rai, soca, and salsa concerts. The question is, why have these traditions succeeded where other European folk music has declined in appeal?

Hungary is like its music. It seems an extremely cosmopolitan, very European country. Budapest is the quintessential *mittel-Europa* city, reminding visitors from the West what the wonderful flavour of urban life was like before the advent of steel and glass office buildings and chain stores. But the language and look of the people bear no relation to those of their Slavic and Germanic neighbours. You can search in vain amid unfamiliar combinations of vowels and consonants for any

(Opposite) Zoltán Kodály – composer and musical archivist

recognisable Latin, Germanic or Slavic root. Even their linguistic second cousins from Finland and Turkey find the language impossible to understand.

The Hungarians originally came from Asia and their looks bear testimony to this. With high cheekbones and dark complexions, they are everyone's romantic idea of Taras Bulba. They are Magyars, not Huns, but they followed Atilla into the vacuum created by his invasion and settled on the Danubian plains. From the ninth to the fourteenth century they dominated the Slavic people around them. The traditions of the great years of Magyar kings remain ever-present in Hungarian lore and national pride. Eventually they were absorbed into the Ottoman Empire and then the Austrian. National feelings have remained strong and the totemic modern dates are the risings of 1848 and 1956; both were suppressed by Russian troops.

Many people feel they know about Hungarian music – all gypsy violins and cymbals. They may even have been to Budapest and heard it there, so it must surely have been authentic. Unfortunately, the sentimental melodies most often heard, dripping with retards and usually played in Hungarian restaurants, bear as much resemblance to traditional Hungarian music as The Gipsy Kings do to real flamenco.

The music *looks* familiar – violins, a bass, and perhaps a bagpipe or a cymbal. But once the rhythm starts, you realise that nothing in European music even remotely resembles it. The metre is slurred, the notes start before the beat, and the beautiful melodies begin like those in Celtic music, but then wander into totally unexpected and delightfully illogical phrases (at least that's how it sounds to Western ears). Like most folk music, its form originated in the rituals of village life. For example, wedding dances start with a slow, sensual dance and evolve, sometimes over a period of several hours, to faster and faster tempi.

Faint echoes of some of the rhythmic feel of the music can be found in Franz Liszt's works, but the real pioneers in the formalisation of Hungarian music were Béla Bartók and Zoltán Kodály. Even before Cecil Sharpe and Vaughan Williams were making similar sorties into the English countryside, Bartók and Kodály were out in Transylvania

with notebook and wire recorder. Some of their original recordings have been reissued and you can hear stark, haunting versions of the two composers' most famous melodies played on a single fiddle, bagpipe or whistle by a shepherd at the turn of the century.

The fierce musical nationalism of Liszt, Bartók and Kodály was inspired in part by the limitations placed on Hungarian freedom by the Hapsburg Empire. It might stretch a point to trace the origins of 'tans haus' (dance house) folk revival of the late nineteen-sixties and seventies to the repression of the Hungarian rising of 1956, but it is hard to deny the intensity of national feeling which unites the folk movement and the anti-Russian sentiments of much of the population. By the early seventies you could find, on any night in Budapest, a room full of young students and intellectuals dancing wildly to the rhythms of Hungarian village music. In form, the sort of circle dances they would do are reminiscent of the folk dances seen at gatherings of earnest folk enthusiasts in London or New York. In the West, such dances are cold and formal. But when played by young Hungarians they are extremely sensuous.

Many different sorts of musicians became drawn to folk music; classical players depressed by the narrow-mindedness of the academies, and rock and jazz musicians looking for something more unique in their own culture. The early recordings of the revival groups are naive and not highly skilled, but groups such as Muzsikas and Sipos began visiting Transylvania, collecting songs and melodies and learning the instrumental styles of the village musicians. In time they came to combine an authenticity of style with an urban sophistication and a highly evolved technique.

All these musicians revered the work of Bartók and Kodály and tended to follow in their footsteps on their collecting trips. Another Kodály connection emerged in the person of the first real star of the dance house movement – Martá Sebestyén. Her mother is a high school music teacher who studied under Kodály. She has devoted her life to teaching Hungarian children about their musical heritage and her daughter was certainly well schooled in these traditions from an early age. She began singing in the mid-seventies and by the early eighties was established as the leading

(Background) Hungarian uprising 1956. A huge statue of Stalin is broken up in a display of anti-Russian sentiment and (opposite) village musicians in Hungary, early this century

vocalist of the movement.

Ironically, as Muzsikas and other groups from Hungary such as Vujicsics and Zsarotnok became increasingly well known, the level of interest in Hungary itself declined. Dance houses have closed, as weekly meetings are attended by fewer and fewer dancers. But the interest of Western countries in the music has meant that Hungarians who were never involved in the dance house movement are now beginning to take a new look at their own folk music.

In the winter of 1987, I saw a remarkable performance by the Kodály Dance Ensemble accompanied by Martá and Muzsikas. It started with a very modern piece set to electronic music. The theme of the dances was censorship and repression, given expression through a very striking example of modern dance theatre. Suddenly the stage was filled with men and women in traditional costume mingling to the distinctive sound of the plucked kontra and the bowed bass of Muzsikas. The men and women paired off and began a beautiful wedding dance. Nothing could have been further from what had gone before. I had been surprised by the political aggressiveness of the modern pieces, but my companions were astonished by the traditional piece. The whole audience seemed stunned. It was then explained to me that it was a traditional song about the wedding guest who had refused to leave: 'You have drunk up all the wine, eaten all the food, now it is time you left'.

Folk musicians are often intensely involved in two political issues in Hungary. One is the movement towards democracy and the loosening of ties with the Soviet Union. The other, even more emotive issue, is Transylvania. Transylvania is an area of Romania which is mostly Hungarian speaking. It was taken from Hungary after the First World War and given to Romania. The Romanian government of Nicolai Caescescu is currently trying to wipe out all traces of Hungarian culture from the region. Musically and culturally, Transylvania is like the American Deep South — the source of the truest expression of the oldest traditions of the culture. It is as if the area from Texas to North Carolina had been given to Mexico following a lost war, and the Mexicans were imposing the Spanish language in all schools, and banning blues, and country and western. Having visited Transylvania many times on collecting trips, Hungarian folk revival musicians are often the leading witnesses to what is happening in the area, and are also in the vanguard of protests against the moves by Romania to destroy thousands of villages and move the peasants to urban centres.

Perhaps it is the intensity of national pride which gives the music its appeal. Comparing the coarse nationalism of British football hooligans with the unashamed pride Hungarians take in their culture and their dedication to retaining as much of it as they can in music, language and craft, one can only be shamed by the shallowness of some of what passes for national pride in Western cultures.

Bulgaria

To travel to Sofia from Budapest is to enter a different world. The mood here is a mixture of the Mediterranean, the Slavic, and the Middle Eastern, and the music of Bulgaria is just as strange to Western European ears.

The village music of Bulgaria is remarkably varied for such a small country. In the Bulgarian quintennial festival at Koprivshtitsa, there are separate stages for each of nine or ten separate districts, each with a style and a musical language of its own. Together they make up one of the richest lodes of traditional music still existing in Europe.

There are many theories about the complexity of the folklore tradition and the unique style of singing for which the country is known. Certainly in ancient times Thracians were reputed to be great musicians – Orpheus was one after all. According to most Bulgarians, the real foundry of their music was the 500 years of Turkish rule, when all expressions of the culture were forced underground. Instead of being destroyed by this, Bulgarian music emerged strengthened. It is almost like a rich vein of precious metal formed by the collision of two continental plates – Asian and European. The wail of the voices and bagpipes have an oriental feel about them, while the melodies and song structures are clearly part of a European folk tradition. One intriguing footnote to the Ottoman occupation was their resettling in central Bulgaria of a large group of Georgians from the northeast borders of the empire. Georgians have a strong tradition of vocal choirs and a style not entirely unlike the Bulgarians. Whether there is a key to *Le Mystère De Voix Bulgares* in this obscure fact will never be known for certain.

Following five centuries of Ottoman rule, there was an outpouring of pride in the national culture, preserved for so long under such difficult conditions. This emerged interestingly in 1946 when Bulgaria became a signatory to the Warsaw pact and joined the Socialist Bloc of Eastern Europe. Whereas many of their allies were rather wary of encouraging too much national pride, since the expression of that pride was often full of anti-Russian sentiments, the Bulgarians were free to sponsor it with unreserved enthusiasm. After

(Opposite) Franz Liszt, Hungarian composer and (above) Béla Bartók playing a peasant hurdy-gurdy

83

all, the historic enemy was not Russia but Turkey, and Russia had helped to free Bulgaria from the Turkish yoke, even against the wishes of Britain and France.

In 1951, Bulgaria, like other Socialist countries, started a national folklore ensemble modelled on Soviet groups like Moysiev or the Red Army Chorus. The dubious philosophy of these ensembles was to glorify the 'people's music' by presenting it in the grandest and most overbearing way possible; size and pomp took precedence over quality. One could speculate on the numerous political and psychological implications in such a trend, which glorifies the people while at the same time regimenting and controlling their music through the formal arrangements. In other countries such as Hungary, the result is the kind of show that tends to play in the West to coach parties of suburban matrons and nostalgic immigrants. Bulgaria struck lucky, however, in choosing Philip Koutev as director for its national ensemble.

Koutev can truly be said to be a kind of Bulgarian Kodály or Bartók, save that he hasn't taken the folk music he collected all the way back to the conservatory as they did in Hungary. He based his settings of traditional songs around the harmonies of village music. Strictly speaking, Bulgarian music has no harmonies in the Western sense. Much of the music is based on the drone, whether it be the fixed 'bourdon' note of the gaida bagpipe, the resonant strings behind the melody strings of the gadulka fiddle, or the vocal 'bourdon' held by two or more women while another sings the melody. The resulting harmonies often involve impossibly close intervals. With a standard European vocal technique, these intervals would produce an unbearable dissonance. Bulgarian vocal technique, however, uses the 'open throat' style, in which the note is delivered powerfully from the head, not the diaphragm, and is therefore pure with no inherent vibrato. This enables 'seconds' and even closer intervals to be thrilling and haunting without ever sounding ugly.

Koutev's genius lay in his ability to write arrangements incorporating the intervals unique to Bulgarian music and the 'open throat' techniques unique to its singers into arrangements which also utilise Western classical harmonies. The result is not pure folk tradition, but a refinement just as interesting as the orchestrations of Bartók or the formalisations of tradition found in classical flamenco.

He went throughout the countryside auditioning singers and instrumentalists. Then he wrote arrangements using the regional styles of the soloists to advantage, keeping the individual qualities of the different districts in the lead part and enriching the usual instrumental accompaniment with his own harmonies taken from classical and religious music.

It is not just good marketing that led Marcel Cellier to call his volumes of archive recordings *Le Mystère des Voix Bulgares*. It does seem likely that much of Europe, in the Middle Ages, used to sing in a style close that of the Bulgarians. A number of leading early music experts have sent singers to Bulgaria to study the style with a view to developing a more authentic recreation of medieval styles of singing.

What is unarguable is the broad appeal of the style. The Radio Choir has now toured the United States and northern Europe, and the ensemble Balkana which includes musicians and singers from both the Radio Ensemble and the Koutev Ensemble has toured Britain, Europe and America to full houses. Kate Bush has recorded three tracks on her latest LP with the Trio Bulgarka, using the style of arrangements heard on their recordings and that of the choir. Inspired by pictures on the front page of Bulgarian newspapers of Yanka Rupkina from the Trio Bulgarka kissing George Harrison, there has been a surge of interest in folk music in Bulgaria, just as it was beginning to lose ground with young audiences, particularly in the cities.

Lest it be felt that Bulgarian music is eventually destined for some kind of audio museum or to be preserved by skilled urban revivalists as it is in Hungary, there is now a new phenomenon sweeping the countryside and cities alike – the wedding band.

I first met the king of the wedding bands, clarinetist Ivo Papasov, at a performance by the Plovdiv Folk-Jazz Ensemble in Sofia. The group marks an attempt to integrate Bulgarian melodies and harmonies into a rather dated jazz-rock style. Most of the musicians are academy-schooled jazz

(Background) Béla Bartók on one of his field trips recording folk songs, Hungary 1908. (Opposite top) Traditional village band. Ocsa village, Hungary and (opposite bottom) Martá Sebestyén and Muzsikas

84

fans and the result is rather pedestrian, or at least it was, until Papasov came on as a featured soloist. His wild, fluid and aggressive playing instantly transformed the proceedings. Afterwards I asked if he had a band of his own. There was general laughter – his Trakia Orchestra is the best-known band in Bulgaria with the possible exception of the FSB, the leading heavy rock outfit.

Two days later, I found myself in a village on the Thracian plain, under the shadow of the Rhodope Mountains in Central Bulgaria. A tent had been put up and was filling with long tables piled high with food, beer and wedding gifts. The guests were almost entirely gypsies. The music began at noon and continued for twelve hours until midnight. It marked all the traditional rituals of the wedding with the appropriate horo, ratchenitsa, buchimich or other unusual rhythms in 5/8, 7/8 or 11/16. The speed, agility and sheer volume of the band was beyond anything heard in traditional Bulgarian music. The line-up was clarinet, saxophone, electric guitar, gadulka, accordion and drum kit. The drummer was a cross between Dave Mattacks (of Fairport Convention) and the jazz drummer Billy Cobham, accentuating his strict dance time-keeping with a dazzling jazz technique. The saxophonist honked and riffed, propelling the dancers as if it were roadhouse honky-tonk in Memphis. It was, in short, overwhelming.

Papasov is from southern Thrace near the Greek and Turkish borders and he and his father before him both played the zorna – a Middle Eastern horn which has now been replaced in most bands by the clarinet. As a clarinetist, he has few peers in Europe. He has listened avidly to the music of all the cultures surrounding Bulgaria – Greek, Turkish, Serbian and Macedonian, as well as to people like Charlie Parker and Benny Goodman. The resulting hybrid has become the most popular music in the countryside and is beginning to challenge rock in the cities. The Bulgarian authorities have been slow to approve this new trend since many of the musicians are from gypsy or Turkish-speaking families and many of the melodies in the early days of wedding bands were considered 'non-Bulgarian'. Now, however, there is a festival competition for wedding bands every year at Stambolovo – hence the new category of 'Stambolovo bands'.

The growing interest in the West in these Stambolovo bands and the surprise of audiences at concerts who came to hear the female singers and stayed to marvel at the instrumentalists lead me to speculate that the coming years will see as much interest in the instrumental music of Bulgaria as there has been up to now in its vocal music. This, though, begs a bigger question: is there a future for indigenous European music in the face of Afro-American dominance?

Certainly, the past decade has seen three trends. The first might be referred to as the 'ECM' factor. European labels have long been in the vanguard of jazz documentation, but for years they were mostly concerned with recording black American jazz musicians overlooked by American companies. Then came the success of ECM's policy of recording European jazz players whose allegiance was as much to European folk and classical traditions as it was to American jazz forms. The fact that this has led indirectly to the vapid noodlings of 'new age' music should not obscure the fact that there is a new form emerging from European musicians who have learnt their techniques from jazz but are bringing non-African melodies and harmonies to the forefront of their music. This trend can be seen in the work of Jan Gabarek at one extreme and Ivo Papasov at the other.

The second observable trend is the way countries newly exposed to Western pop embrace it at first with an enthusiasm which leads many to fear for the survival of local forms. When I first visited Spain twenty years ago, I was considered eccentric by my friends for wanting to hear flamenco when there were so many jazz and rock concerts around. Now Spaniards seek out old flamenco greats just as Americans hunted down obscure blues artists during the sixties. The popularity of the Trio Bulgarka in Bulgaria is also beginning a new surge of interest among young, urban Bulgarians in the traditional music of their own culture. It seems that if the fascination with Afro-American rhythms doesn't exactly wear off, it certainly tends to dissipate somewhat after a period.

The third trend concerns the growing disillusionment of Western audience with pop. For years pop was a broad church, with something for everyone, full of interesting avant-garde forms to satisfy the most adventurous tastes. But now the niche once occupied by punk, protest or fusion is filled by music from all over the world; soca, salsa, and soukous, Tibetan and Mongolian chanting, and Zulu choirs. Western music consumers have been ever thus. They require periodic injections of musical stimulation, since the urban bourgeois culture does not contain the rituals and texture of life necessary to produce intense musical rhythms. The excitement in early nineteenth-century ballrooms was provided by the waltz, which was as controversial in its day as the twist was 150 years later. There is nothing new about the West plundering the music of other cultures to enliven its own music. What makes this era so interesting is the speed of communications, leading to the devouring of styles at a much faster rate than ever before, and to the feedback of the new amalgams into the original source culture.

It is easy to overemphasise the power of the Coca-Cola culture of the West. In figures like Martá Sebestyén, Ivo Papasov, and thousands like them all over the world, there is enough talent and dedication to inspire the preservation of musical traditions and to create new developments which are the lifeblood of any music. It seems that only Western pop is stagnating at the moment. Hungary and Bulgaria are bursting with energy and talent for the world to enjoy in future years.

(Opposite centre) Village musician playing the gadulka and (opposite bottom) the picture that inspired a surge of interest in Bulgarian folk music, George and Yanka.
(This page top) The Trio Bulgarka and (bottom) Ivo Papasov (second from left standing) – King of Stambolovo

NEW SONG-

MUSIC AND POLITICS IN LATIN AMERICA

JAN FAIRLEY

In Latin America music matters because it is intimately bound up with the social and political life of the continent. Since the time of the troubadours who accompanied the Spanish conquistadores, since the ballads of the Mexican revolution, it is in the music of the Americas that the history of the ordinary people is written. Most important has been live performance, whether it is the small *pena* (music club) or the stadium concert. And much of this music has dealt with life and death issues. To give just one example: after the fall of the military dictatorship in Argentina in 1983, when national rock singer Victor Heredia came on stage and sang

'We are still singing, we are still demanding, we are still dreaming, we are still hoping ... where have they taken them?' it was to an audience which was aware that the singer himself, like many of those present, numbered an immediate family member as one of those who 'disappeared' during the dark years of the internal 'dirty war'.

The Argentinian experience is not unique. Audiences in Latin America tend to participate with a passion and commitment equal to that of the artist. Audience and performers are united in a close relationship through songs and their spoken introductions.

In 1967, the Cuban *Encuentro de la Cancion*

Protesta (Protest Song Meeting) first brought a generation of Latin American musicians together in one place. Here many, but by no means all, who were just starting out as singer/songwriters had the chance to listen to each others' music and discuss the different situations in each country. A few years earlier Argentine Mercedes Sosa and others produced a manifesto advocating a new song and poetry to match the times. Their aims were summed up in Cesar Isella and Tejada Gomez's 'Cancion con todos' ('Song for All'):

> I go out to walk
> the cosmic belt of the south
> ... all the blood can become a song in the wind
> sing with me sing
> brother American
> free your hope with a cry in your voice.

The desire for exchange and unity in Latin America, celebrated by musicians since 1967 under the guise of a loose movement called 'new song', is not in fact something new. We should remember that Latin America (save for Brazil) was colonised by one country – Spain. It was liberated by one army led by leaders from various countries working together. Prominent among them was Simon Bolivar of Venezuela whose expressed aim was to unite the continent. When Che Guevara tried to stimulate a continental movement from a base in Bolivia in 1967, such unity again became a major issue. Latin America has always been a land possessed and exploited by outsiders. The desire for unity is founded on the realisation that only by individual countries standing together can the continent survive.

Although the Cuban meeting was organised around the idea of protest, that term is wholeheartedly rejected by the musicians themselves. While many songs written over the years have directly or indirectly made reference to political events, the majority have remained reflective, expressing several themes in many different ways and often intertwining love and personal relations with feelings about home and country. It is significant that the majority of musicians have no direct links with political parties (although many have worked with them at particular times). What draws them together is a common passion for, and commitment to, the fate of the individual, of their country and of their continent. This often takes the form of a search for identity which fuses the personal with the collective.

This idea of searching is encapsulated in one of the peerless recordings of the eighties Panamanian salsa singer Ruben Blades. *Buscando America* (*Searching for America*) became a hit all over the continent (and in North America). Traditionally, salsa, like tango, has largely been concerned with wronged men and treacherous women, lost love, and the familiar problems of life in the barrio. Blades took salsa into another realm, wrapping up in the track order of the record a contemporary narrative of the Americas. The present struggles of the continent are skilfully represented in cameos of everyday life.

Blades himself has confirmed that the order of the record tracks (and their juxtaposition) is intended to resolve ambiguities inherent in songs as individual items: so it moves from 'Decisions', following the fate of the pregnant schoolgirl and the drunk who thinks he can beat the truck and the lights; through the witty but sinister monologue 'GBDB' of a member of the secret police/death squad carrying out his daily morning routine; to 'Disappearances'; to a version of the Peruvian waltz 'Everyone Returns'; to the plight of refugees in 'Green Roads'; to the struggle in El Salvador and the murder of the Bishop who championed the rights of ordinary people over the state; and finally to the search for America herself (neither north nor south):

> I'm searching for America and I fear I won't find her
> ... I'm calling America but she doesn't reply
> those who fear truth have hidden her
> ... while there is no justice there can be no peace
> ... if the dream of one is the dream of all let's break the chains and begin to walk
> ... I'm calling you, America, our future awaits us before we all die help me find her.

Just as the 1967 Cuban meeting was partly organised in an attempt to break Cuba's cultural isolation, so in 1983 a Central American Peace Concert, held in Managua, Nicaragua, became an act of public support for Nicaragua at a time when international solidarity was beginning to wane. The live recording of the event, *April in Managua*, captures the atmosphere of that day in the Square

(Opposite) Mercedes Sosa – Argentinian singer. One of the founders of the 'new song' movement

outside the palace where the Sandinistas had over-thrown the dictator Somoza. The presence of musicians from all over the Americas broke the ring of silence around Nicaragua. In common with so many live recordings around this time, when musicians from various countries took part together, the participation of the crowd was crucial.

Love songs apart, Nicaraguan musicians would seem to subscribe to the Brechtian notion that art is a hammer that forges society. With the help of musicians in Mexico, the Godoy brothers recorded songs which were broadcast on the radio from the guerrilla zones. Using folk forms, they told how to make molotov cocktails; and how to take apart, clean, load and fire an M-1 rifle. Song became a direct form of intervention; a direct means of communication with the largely illiterate populace. Later, song was used in the Sandinistas' literacy campaigns. And when wheat became scarce, following the US economic embargo, songs like 'We Want Bread With Dignity' were used to remind people that wheat was the oldest form of food in the Americas.

The Nicaraguan Peace Concert finished with Mercedes Sosa's 'Cuando Tenga La Tierra' ('When the Land is Ours'), reminding everyone once again that land, and the possession of land, has been an issue in South America since the Spaniards arrived in 1492. That moment is universally regarded as the beginning of a continuing history of inter-vention in the lives of the ordinary people of the continent.

Mexico's Amparo Ochoa and the Folkoristas definitive interpretation of fellow countryman Gabino Palomares' 'Malinche's Curse', perhaps one of the most significant songs of the 'new song' movements on the continent, brings that moment to life:

> We watched them come from the sea
> my feathered brothers were the bearded men of
> the awaited prophecy
> we heard the voice of the monarch that God had
> arrived
> and we opened the door out of fear of the unknown
> they came mounted on beasts
> like evil demons
> covered in metal
> with fire in their hands

(Background) Daniel Ortega. Leader of the Sandinistas and President of Nicaragua

... Today we still exchange gold for trinkets and glass beads ... today we still open doors to the white man and call him friend
yet when we see an Indian, wearily walking down from the mountains
we humiliate him, treat him as a stranger in his own land.

The musical arrangement interacts with the lyric, mapping the historic process: first the sound of indigenous shakers, shells, seeds, prehistoric flutes and bones, with drums slowly added; then the European strings the Spanish brought with them, early guitars, mandolins, lauds, lutes, harps, fiddles and the local versions of string instruments adapted to local aesthetics and made with armadillo shells and wood. The underlying rhythm moves from acoustic percussion to the swinging *mestizo* dance rhythms of this century, but with the primordial flute ever present.

Since the very beginning, therefore, much of Latin American music has been part of a culture of resistance. The wealth of the New World — whether it be land, or the gold and silver of the Aztecs, Mayans and Incas — was plundered to sustain the old. And foreigners have not been the only group to take possession of the land and its riches. The bourgeoisie of each country, under-using land and denying basic rights to the people that work it, have played their part. In 1966, Uruguayan singer Daniel Viglietti could be confident that:

If my song bothers you
or someone close by
I'm sure it'll be a foreigner
or a Uruguayan landowner
... the earth is ours
... Pedro's, Maria's
Juan's and Jose's.

In 1968, Chilean Victor Jara sang 'Questions about Puerto Montt', only days after the bloody killing by government troops of homeless people who had seized unused land in the south of Chile.

One live concert, above all others, entwined the themes of land and sacrifice. 'Corazon Americano' ('American Heart') united Brazilian Milton Nascimento with Mercedes Sosa and fellow Argentine Leon Gieco in Brazil in 1984. In both countries the young people have borne the brunt of waves of repression. The songs performed then embrace the recurrent themes of so much Latin American song and poetry, which revolve around the relationship between the land, the seed, crops like wheat and maize and, in this concert, honey. Through these metaphors is communicated the massive sacrifice of youth under a military regime. Honey represents the sweetness of life. The seed becomes a symbol of the rebirth of those lost, a child perhaps, or a dead activist or simply one of the thousands of 'missing' bodies buried in unmarked graves. To harvest each piece of wheat is to reclaim the lost. Not only do the people have the right to life and to possession of their land but the land and the people are seen as one and the same.

If the development of a culture of resistance can be traced back to the arrival of the Spanish conquistadores, the rapid spread of Western cultural values in the fifties was what sparked the musicians and writers of the new song movements. Alarmed by the fact that local artists were taking North American names and mimicking what they heard on the radio, they drew parallels between early Spanish colonisation and the new invaders, and looked to preHispanic culture as a sign and symbol of real root identity.

The end of the fifties marked a significant first stage. Key figures like Atahualpa Yupanqui in Argentina, Carlos Puebla in Cuba, and Violeta Parra in Chile, brought the musical traditions of the countryside to the city, making them available to a new generation and adapting them to suit the mood of the times. Puebla sang country music with satirical lyrics, Parra produced her famous 'La Carta' ('The Letter') which describes the news that reached her in Paris about the imprisonment of her brothers for striking. Yupanqui wrote 'Basta, ya' which became little short of a hymn for the next generation. 'The Yankees have pushed us around for long enough! The Yankees have been in charge long enough.'

Their music stimulated student musical groups as well as the singer/songwriters. In Chile, for example, in the years preceding the election of Salvador Allende as President, groups emerged playing music of the communities of the Andean *altiplano* where the culture of the indigenous people of the Americas has resisted erosion for centuries. These groups took Indian names like Inti Illimani (Sun Over Illimani, a Bolivian mountain) and wore the ponchos of workers. In this way, the student was linked with the worker and the peasant; the countryside with the town. The students and the intellectuals saw themselves as the active link between the peasantry and the urban workers. Musically they brought together instruments and rhythms, which until then had been associated with quite separate musical traditions, to make one strong Latin American statement. This was most apparent in their mixing together of Andean pipes, Spanish and vernacular strings, Indian drums, and Afro-Caribbean percussion.

After the Chilean coup d'état of 1973 there were severe repercussions. Victor Jara was killed, other musicians were imprisoned and groups like Inti Illimani and Quilapayun spent fifteen years marooned in exile ('the longest tour in the history of Chilean music'). Many years after prominent trade unionists and politicians had been allowed back, they remained on Pinochet's lists of those denied the right to return. Their music maintained the culture of resistance in exile and became the heart and soul of soli-

darity movements abroad, raising funds for survival inside and emotionally sustaining those forced to remain outside. When Inti Illimani were finally given permission to return, they sang 'I return, without asking for pardon, nor to be forgotten' to the 5000 people who greeted them at the airport.

Rock *nacional* in Argentina, particularly in the period preceding and during the Falklands War, provides the most remarkable example of what we might call a culture not only of resistance but of survival. Singer Charly Garcia became a leading spokesman for the young who suffered the double impact of the internal dirty war and the Falklands campaign. As he sang in 'Alice's Song in the Country':

The innocent are guilty
Says his highness, the King of Spades.

With meetings of any sort prohibited, the con-

certs of the national rock movement became important free spaces, a 'region of poetry and music', where young people could meet, although not in complete safety, since police were waiting outside ready to add names to the list of the disappeared. In the words of one concert-goer: 'Outside black reality, bloody declarations of war, dead; inside love, guitars, long hair.' The cry which had everyone jumping on their seats at concerts inside stadiums was 'El que no salta es un militar' ('If you're not jumping you're a soldier').

Outside the concerts, the music of the rock movement circulated via cassettes. Small groups met to listen together. There was a proliferation of fanzines which charted the period through the words of their public, particularly *Imaginary Express*. Music was a collective experience, a form of survival; as one person said succinctly, a way of 'saving identity'. 'They want to take our spirit away, they want to kill us.'

With the Falklands War, youth status changed. No longer 'delinquent', they were hailed as the saviours of their country and sacrificed on a large scale. Ironically, the decision of the authorities not to transmit any more music in English meant that for the first time national rock secured massive coverage on radio and television. In an attempt to undercut its impact, the military tried to co-opt the movement and invited rock stars to take part in concerts for the war. Instead, the musicians mounted a Festival of Latin American Solidarity which turned itself into an anti-War event; those who attended directly contributed to the needs of the young men sent to fight by bringing sweaters and cigarettes. Leon Gieco summed up the mood of both the Festival and the time with his magnificent song 'Solo le pido a Dios':

I only ask God
not to make me indifferent to war
It is a great monster that tramples on
the poor innocence of the people.

Today, the situation in most Latin American countries has changed from the dark days of

(Above) Chilean singer Victor Jara, executed during the military coup of 1973 and (opposite) Atahualpa Yupanqui

dictatorship. Those who sang songs of struggle, resistance and survival have now to adapt to the complexities of living in new democracies. What will the people of Uruguay, Brazil, Argentina and Chile require of their musicians as the continent moves into the nineties?

One indication might be found in the work of singer/songwriter Silvio Rodriguez who has been searching for ways to maintain a position of critical independence in post-Revolutionary Cuba. Rodriguez may still sing 'Vivo en un Pais Libre' ('I Live in a Free Country'), and celebrate the Revolution's achievements, but he also alludes subtly to its disappointments and frustrations. His songs speak not only to a Cuban audience but also to young people all over the continent and beyond. Perhaps more than anyone else, Rodriguez has succeeded in reflecting and shaping the feelings and aspirations of a new generation of Latin Americans.

Around midnight on the 27 January 1989, Rodriguez, accompanied by fellow musicians Afro Cuba, sound and lighting technicians, a tour production team, stage hands, roadies, members of the Cuban Press, television and radio, and scores of young people who had gathered from all over the island, began an arduous climb of the Pico Turquino, the highest point in the Sierra Maestra mountains in Cuba. The day chosen for the climb was the 136th anniversary of the birth of Cuba's national poet, Jose Marti. His statue stands on the top of the peak. Marti was a leading intellectual and activist, responsible for the independence movement which operated from this area against the Spanish in 1895. These mountains are also where Fidel Castro, Che Guevara and the other leaders of the Revolution fought as guerrillas in the fifties to overthrow Batista, the corrupt ruler of the island.

At the top of the peak of Turquino, in brilliant sunshine, Rodriguez sang a small selection of music of the old and new *trova* traditions. His songs fused the personal and the political, his own origins and those of the Cuban Revolution, subtly combining intimate personal experience with the movement of history and politics. Most of them could be best described as love songs and were rich in complex imagery. Much of Rodriguez's material revolves around the search for dreams by each

succeeding generation, and operates on the levels of both metaphor and allegory. These dreams have a surreal quality, whether they concern the loss of perception, the joys of childhood, or serpents who consume you, forcing you to fight from within. In a song called 'The Prison', dedicated to the time Castro and his comrades were imprisoned before the Revolution, he tells his audience that:

The prison is over
    the prison of iron
        but the prison of dreams
            continues.

Rodriguez speaks of his music as 'a little like following the line of the horizon, knowing that the nearer it seems, there will always be a place further away to get to, and the hope of finding that place is even further away.' Ultimately, perhaps, the tremendous appeal of his music lies in his ability to capture what Oriente Lopez, the young musical director of Afro Cuba, has described as 'a culture of dreams'. Four hundred years of colonial intervention in Latin America has left behind 'a sort of impossibility, of wanting and dreaming the impossible'. For Rodriguez, wanting the impossible has its positive aspect. He understands too that his dreams cannot be the dreams of future generations. Times change. His young audience have their own aspirations and they will move forward.

As we move into the nineties, it is not in novels, poetry, plays or films that the most telling reflection of young people's experience in the Americas will be found. For that we must continue to look to singers like Silvio Rodriguez.

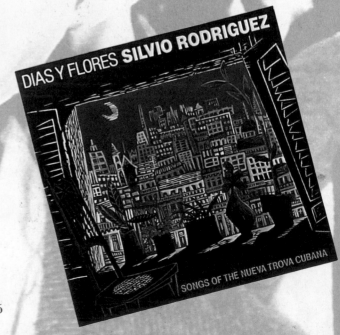

(Background) Mothers of 'The Disappeared'. (Above) Silvio Rodriguez and (opposite) Argentinian soldiers huddled against the wind during the Falklands War

96

SOUTH AFRICA-
MUSIC IN THE SHADOWS
ROB PRINCE

'Y ou know, things work out quite psychologically in South Africa. Anything that has been outside South Africa creates a real interest. Now, every newspaper in South Africa is writing about Mahlathini.'

Sipho Mabuse sips his coffee and gazes through the hotel window at the busy street outside. It's a beautiful sunny morning in London, and Mabuse, a leading figure in South Africa's township music scene, is in transit between Brussels (where he has been producing a new album for South African singer, Miriam Makeba) and Soweto, his home town.

For young, sophisticated, politically aware musicians like Mabuse, Mahlathini's international success is welcome, but not without irony, because the mbaqanga township jive of Mahlathini and The Mahotella Queens is no longer the beat on the street in the townships. 'What the world appreciates in South African music is not what is actually appreciated *in* the country,' muses the singer with a wry smile. 'It really does create a lot of difficulties for musicians like myself, who work internationally.'

His sentiment is echoed by Johnny Clegg, a white South African musician playing a modern synthesis of township music and rock. Says Clegg:

(Opposite) Mahlathini – the Lion of Soweto

A whole new young musical crew has grown up in South Africa. They're playing a reggae, mbaqanga, techno-pop, disco crossover, and they're singing in English. They regard mbaqanga as slave music, music that was played by their fathers. They want to progress as musicians and get beyond that, but they feel bound by the music form that's been hailed internationally.

The frustrations of young South African musicians like Clegg and Mabuse, who desperately want to present a modern, sophisticated sound to the world, and yet find the world responding to music they find old-fashioned, says as much about the current state of music outside South Africa as it does about the South African music scene itself. To the music fan in the West, Mahlathini's music offers a rough-edged spontaneity absent in the electronic rhythms of commercial pop. There is real experience here, a rhythm of resistance, an indestructible beat. But in the townships of South Africa, white Anglo-Saxon preoccupations with authenticity count for little. These days, on the dusty streets that spawned mbaqanga, Michael Jackson is more of a role model than Mahlathini. For the youths in the townships, mbaqanga is not simply old-fashioned; it carries with it political connotations that have so far registered only dimly in the West. To them mbaqanga is the music of acquiescence. Its lyrics, which hark back to tribal traditions, or address the everyday problems of township life, do not sit well with the mood of militancy that has swept the townships since the Soweto uprising of 1976. Though lately there are signs that a re-evaluation may be under way – part of the 'psychology' that Sipho Mabuse observes – notions of black pride and consciousness have nevertheless tended to draw on American models, rather than traditional tribal values.

The affinity with American culture has been a recurring factor in the development of township music. As early as the twenties, marabi, the popular music of the township shebeens (illegal drinking dens) included a strong, Dixieland jazz influence, filtered through European and African tribal elements. As jazz trumpeter-in-exile, Hugh Masekela explains:

South Africa was a highly industrialised society from the turn of the century. So all the fancy wares from overseas were reaching us, including gramophones and records, instruments and all that. So we had access to an African-American culture, and African-Americans were role models: we had so many people called 'Satch' and 'Duke' in the townships.

Marabi, the earliest identifiable manifestation of township music, was very much a working-class style. Its mongrel combination of urban (jazz) and traditional (ethnic) was strongly disapproved of by the small bourgeois elite of educated blacks who expressed a preference for pure, unadulterated American jazz. Their tastes were amply catered for during the thirties and forties by township big bands like the Jazz Maniacs and the Harlem Swingsters, who did a fair job of slavishly recreating the American sound. These bands, who would dress in tuxedos and, according to Masekela, 'play all the licks', were popular with (segregated) white audiences, as well as with township blacks. But no matter how accurate their renditions of Glen Miller, Duke Ellington, Count Basie or Cab Calloway, hints of marabi were never far beneath the surface.

American dances and fashions, like the jitterbug (jive) and the 'zoot suit', became essential accessories to the music. The zoot suit, a baggy-trousered three-piece popular with streetwise American blacks, was a favoured style with young township blacks seeking street credibility, and also lent itself to a new slang term, 'tsotsi' (from the African pronunciation of zoot suit), meaning 'teddy boy' or 'street thug'. During the forties and fifties, gangs of knife-wielding tsotsis developed the habit of using jazz concerts as battle grounds to settle scores – often between rival supporters of one band or musician and another – and the resulting violence eventually contributed to the demise of jazz in South Africa. After the introduction of apartheid in 1948, black jazz musicians found it increasingly difficult to tour and play white clubs and theatres – important sources of income. By the early sixties jazz, as a significant force in South African music, was spent.

Quite why American music had such an impact (elsewhere in Africa, Latin music was the dominant influence) is unclear. Historians have pointed to a similarity between the 'stomp' beat and polyphonic vocals of traditional Zulu music, and the

(Background) Sophiatown, Johannesburg. Black South Africa's unofficial cultural capital in the 1950s and (opposite) Sipho Mabuse – one of the giants of township pop

straight 4/4 rhythm and sophisticated instrumental harmonies of American swing. However, the similarity is probably coincidental, as few if any slaves were transported from South Africa to the Americas. More significant is the strong identification of black South Africans with the black American experience: of slavery and subsequent alienation and exploitation within a white-dominated urban industrial society – an experience that closely parallels black South Africa's own. 'The majority of the people in South Africa are urbanites, not rural,' says Sipho Mabuse, 'so whatever music comes out of South Africa is urban orientated. Even the people in the rural areas today listen to what happens in the cities.'

The balance in favour of the urban contrasts markedly with the rest of Africa, where society remains predominantly rural. Though South Africa's urban black population is largely confined to the periphery of urban centres, in the townships, proximity to a highly developed First World reality has spawned a ghetto culture bearing strong similarities to that of black America. In America, emigration from the rural areas of the South to the ghettoes of the North produced a vibrant cross-fertilisation of musical styles: out of blues and dixieland jazz came R&B, be-bop, and rock'n'roll. A similar process was at work in the townships.

With the enshrinement of apartheid into the constitution came new laws designed to reinforce social divisions along racial and tribal lines, effectively determining where an individual should live according to his or her colour and ethnic background. Tens of thousands of blacks were forcibly moved from one area to another; the flourishing community of Sophiatown, black South Africa's unofficial cultural capital, was destroyed in a military operation, its buildings flattened, its inhabitants despatched 20 km to the south, to what is now Soweto – and all to make way for a new, white suburb.

The resulting social disruption brought a new influx of rural inhabitants into the townships. Their arrival coincided with the wide availability of cheap, mass-produced musical instruments, which the rural immigrants used to play traditional styles in the new way. Zulu guitarists,

for example, retuned the instrument to recreate traditional songs and melodies. By the fifties, Zulu street guitarists were an established feature on the township scene.

At the same time, (white-owned) record companies were waking up to the economic potential of the black, record-buying public – by far the biggest market in South Africa. Penny whistle music, or kwela, a lively blend of jazz, marabi and rural styles that first appeared during the forties, was soon generating massive record sales throughout South Africa. A new commercial jazz style, mbaqanga (not to be confused with the later mbaqanga township jive), which similarly fused elements of marabi and traditional music, also gained popularity, as did mbube, an eclectic mix of traditional Zulu-Swazi and church choral singing, ragtime, and Afrikaans folk styles (the best-known modern exponents are the all-male acapella group, Ladysmith Black Mambazo).

Among the new arrivals from the rural areas was a young penny whistle player named West Nkosi. Nkosi, like many young musicians of the time, had learned to play a flute as a herd boy on his father's farm.

When I was a youngster, about eight or nine, I made a flute from a reed, you know, a reed from the river and I used to play a special tune for the cattle at sunset. I would blow that tune, and all the cattle would group together to go home. After that, I had a feel for other songs singing in my head, and I decided to play them out on that reed.

While still a teenager, Nkosi had run away from home and found work as a domestic servant in Pretoria. Here he met up with three other aspiring domestic servants-cum-music makers, Marks Mankwane, Joseph Makwela and Lucky Monama. They began rehearsing together and eventually wound up at Troubadour Records, where producer and talent scout, Cuthbert Matunga, hired them as session musicians.

At this point the hard-headed logistics of apartheid-style economics took over. At Troubadour, Matunga had established a factory-line operation, achieving maximum turnover by using house musicians to back a stable of 'name' artists. It was, in short, a ruthless hit-making machine, reaping vast profits and offering a meagre flat rate to its hard-working session players. Even top stars

(Background) Sophiatown, Johannesburg, prior to being cleared to make way for a new white suburb.
(Top) Mahlathini and the Mahotella Queens and (opposite) Hugh Masekela

responsible for selling (literally) millions of records were rarely paid royalties. Hugh Masekela likens the situation (then and now) to the Race Records era in America.

It's the same situation, you know, where people stand outside the studio for days, and there's a black representative who comes out and says, 'Okay, you come in.' They call them producers but these guys are just like liaison between the company and the artists, and they get a cut of everything, and half the time the [rural] artist doesn't know anything, and they just pay him the three or four pounds and say, 'your record will be played when we release it'. And then, of course, those musicians make their money from live performing.

Gallo, Troubador's major rival and the leading black record label from the sixties onwards, employed a similar policy. To ensure a smooth operation, Gallo's chief (black) producer and talent scout, Rupert Bopape, would hire rural musicians in preference to urban jazz players, whose creative aspirations and demands for a decent wage he found irksome. Whether intended or not, it was from such primarily economic motivations that a genuine music revolution emerged.

In the hands of the relatively inexperienced and exploited rural musicians, jazz-mbaqanga evolved into a new sound, then still unnamed, that combined marabi and traditional rural styles with a crucial new ingredient: electric instruments. As jazz exited stage left, the tough R&B backbeat of British groups like The Beatles, The Rolling Stones and The Animals, came marching in through the front door.

Into this scenario stepped Simon Nkabinde, aka Mahlathini. In the wake of the Sharpeville Massacre, with an atmosphere of tension and insecurity permeating the townships, the time was right for an epic figure to take centre stage. With his deep, 'goat's voice' vocals, derived from traditional Ngoni praise singing (via Big Voice Jack Lerole, lead singer with the pioneering township jive group, Alexander Black Mambazo) Mahlathini was it.

Bopape was quick to recognise the youngster's potential, signed him up and teamed him with a group of young session musicians newly arrived from Troubadour: West Nkosi (now playing sax), Mankwane (lead guitar), Makwela (bass), Monama (drums), and the late Vivian Ngubane (rhythm guitar). The group became a semi-permanent unit, later dubbing themselves The Makgona Tshole (Jack of All Trades) Band, because as session players, they claimed, they could play anything. A group of female harmony singers, The Mahotella Queens, completed the line-up, allowing Mahlathini to refine the call-and-response style he had developed with the seminal female harmony group, The Dark City Queens.

As befits a mythical character, Mahlathini is careful to preserve a measure of mystique about his persona and background. His name, he claims (one of several differing stories), was taken from the wooded area around the small farmhouse where he was born. 'We were right out in the bushes. So I was called Mahlathini — it means forest.' His 'groaning' or 'goat's voice' vocal style, he recalls, arrived mysteriously when he was eight years old. 'One day I came home, and suddenly I was talking in a deep voice. My mother said, "What's happened to your voice?" And I said, "I don't know". I really don't know what happened.'

After an uncertain start, 'Orlando Train' took the group steaming into the South African charts,

and from then on constant touring and consistent chart success confirmed the band as the leading mbaqanga group of the period. Their brash urban sound (dubbed 'mbaqanga' during a radio interview in the mid-sixties) spawned a legion of imitators and rivals, but none could quite match the potent alchemy of Mahlathini, the Queens and Makgona Tshole together.

In the early seventies, Mahlathini left the band to pursue a solo career. Nkosi moved into production, and The Mahotella Queens continued throughout various personnel changes as a separate unit. But despite the emergence of a new style of soul mbaqanga, spearheaded by the still massively popular Soul Brothers, by the end of the decade mbaqanga had fallen out of fashion. In the post 1976 climate, a new generation, disillusioned with what they saw as the music's reactionary appeal, began to pick up on black American soul and disco. This they considered 'hip' and modern, and also reflective of the black American experience, whose concepts of black pride and consciousness they could identify with. There was also a sense that, inevitably, mbaqanga had run its course. Radio and television, divided throughout the country on strict racial and tribal lines, had little interest in reflecting the cultural or political realities of black urban existence, and mbaqanga was increasingly marginalised as an antiquated form. Saturday night disco-fever was sweeping the world, and South Africans, black and white, wanted to be part of it. White-orientated rock and American soul and disco dominated the airwaves, and white radio, television and record company bosses were on the lookout for a home-grown equivalent with 'international potential'.

Mpantsula musia (aka township pop or township disco), a new hybrid of mbaqanga, reggae and American pop and disco, fitted the bill nicely. Where mbaqanga was rough and uncultured, mpantsula was smooth and safe. It was a civilised sound with consumerist economic vaues (wearing the right clothes, making the right moves) that white media executives could relate to. Better still, it had 'international potential'. By the early eighties, Brenda Fassie, Yvonne Chak-chaka, Super Frika, Stimela, Harari, Jaluka and others had become the new township stars.

With political references reflecting the new

(Background) Children in Alexandra township, Johannesburg and (opposite) Sipho Mchune, one-time collaborator with Johnny Clegg in the band Jaluka

spirit of resistance in the townships (Condry Ziqubu's 'Confusion', Clegg and Savuka's 'Asimbonanga/Mandela'), the new pop-disco fusion has ironically proved more adventurous lyrically than musically. Such instances remain few and far between (Marks Mankwane dismisses the new music as 'nothing but love, love, love') but in the hands of Clegg, Mabuse and others, a new spirit of cultural resistance, reflecting a 'rainbow alliance', transcending racial and tribal barriers, has become apparent. Most strikingly, Johnny Clegg and Savuka – three whites and three blacks on stage together – offers a potent metaphor for South Africa's democratic opposition: a 'shadow culture' that Clegg evokes with eloquence on his album *Shadow Man*. 'The album is about living on the edges and in the shadows,' says Clegg. 'Songs like "Waiting" and "Shadow Man" – every song has that element of the shadow in it, because at the moment, in my country, we're waiting in the shadows, we're living in the shadow of the future.'

The link between music and political opposition in South African began early in the fifties. Jazz musicians, who were mainly from an urban background, and were thus generally better-educated and informed, began to form a consensus against apartheid. As session players, in white-run theatres, they came into contact with white liberals who were of a like mind. The musical *King Kong*, produced by white South African, Ian Bernhardt, was intended as a celebration of black pride (although by non-South African standards the production was considered tame and came in for heavy criticism when it toured the West). Less compromised was the 1957 film *Come Back Africa*, starring jazz-folk singer Miriam Makeba and Soul Brother saxophonist Lemmy 'Special' Mabaso, who appeared as a child prodigy penny whistle player. The film was strongly anti-apartheid and played an important role in creating international awareness of the situation of black people in South Africa for the first time. When Makeba attended the premier of the film at the Venice Film Festival, her citizenship was revoked by the South African government, and she has remained in exile ever since. In America, the singer Harry Belafonte, already an active civil rights campaigner, began to speak out against apartheid, and later helped organise asylum in America for Makeba and Hugh

beat culture, its increasing marginalisation on the music scene coincided with a rise in American-inspired black consciousness. Pioneering this development was a young multi-instrumentalist from Pretoria, Philip Tabane. Tabane began looking to traditional tribal culture not so much as a source of folk wisdom, but as a means of rediscovering a sense of spiritual and musical identity.

In the early sixties, with flautist Abie Cindi, and malombo drummer Julian Bahula, Tabane formed the pioneering Malombo Jazzmen. The Jazzmen's fusion of impressionistic guitar, flute, and rumbling malombo drums (traditionally used to summon up ancestral spirits) proved a highly influential force in South African jazz, pointing the way to a new expression of black pride and consciousness through a powerful evocation of traditional themes, translated into a modern, experimental idiom. The group's concerts often included live poetry as part of the performance, a move which finds a contemporary echo in the work of the political poet, Mzwakhe Mbuli.

In 1965, the Jazzmen parted company. Tabane dropped 'Jazzmen' from the title, and has continued to push back musical barriers with various configurations of his group, most notably in the period 1966–77 with the drummer Gabriel Thobejane, with whom he toured America in the early seventies to great acclaim.

The association between township music and political theatre has also come to a new fruition in the musical *Sarafina* by musician and dramatist, Mbongeni Ngema. Unlike *King Kong*, *Sarafina* is a production that pulls none of its political punches, and has played to enthusiastic audiences on Broadway for a number of years.

But for the moment, within South Africa, the music scene remains as fragmented, and diverse, as it ever was. In the rural areas, and for the older generation in the townships, who are traditionally more conservative (with a small 'c') than their radicalised offspring, the 'old music' – mbaqanga, mbube, Zulu jive – continues to hold tremendous allure. Thus music by Ladysmith Black Mambazo, Sipho Mchune, The Boyoyo Boys, The Soul Brothers, along with new-wave Zulu groups like Amaphisi and bands with a more specifically regional appeal, like the Sotho group Tau Ea

Masekela. Many other talented jazz musicians were to leave South Africa over the next decade, including pianists Dollar Brand and Chris McGregor and saxophonist Dudu Pukwana.

The developing momentum of the black civil rights movement in America, combined with a new, formal experimentalism in jazz pioneered by the likes of John Coltrane, Charlie Mingus and Archie Shepp, found a parallel in South African jazz in the late fifties and early sixties. Whereas before, jazz had been associated with the mainstream, or in the be-bop era with pseudo-American

(Above) Hilda Tloubatla – one of the Mahotella Queens and (opposite) Miriam Makeba

Lesotho (Lion of Lesotho) with its distinctive, bluesy accordion sound, and the 'Cape coloured' group, The Genuines, continue to shift significant numbers of records, but to a far more restricted market than might have been the case fifteen or twenty years ago.

Though there are signs of a revived interest in 'neo-traditional' music, partly as a result of the Mahlathini phenomenon, and partly through a new consciousness of the way apartheid has cynically appropriated tribal culture to promote its own 'homelands' policy, any revival of roots styles is likely to be modest. For the militant youth in the townships, American soul, disco, rap and hip-hop continue to offer a far more cogent and seductive image: that of the contemporary urban (American) black: suave, sophisticated, politically and socially outspoken, economically independent – and *hip*. It's a world in which 'tribal values' and 'roots music' (apart, that is, from roots reggae, whose pan-African Rastafarian message has also had a significant impact) has little rel-evance. In the townships, in surroundings that often lack even the most basic social (not to mention political) facilities, ghetto-blaster culture and the iconography of the American Dream have come to represent the ultimate manifestation of democracy.

With the current state of emergency creating even greater restrictions on freedom of expression and communication than ever before, precisely where South African music will be ten years from now is uncertain. But for those waiting on the edges and in the shadows, in the townships of South Africa, the future is not without hope. As Johnny Clegg insists:

> The South African people are very young, they're very resilient. For me, I take my hope from the people. I don't take it from political anaylsis or from economical or political trends. It take it from the vibe that I get in the street. And the vibe in the street is a ghetto vibe, and it's very positive. It's in the music of the townships.

BLUES FOR THE EIGHTIES

ROBIN DENSELOW

I t's Friday night in the dressing room of a Toronto music joint, and a road manager is leading the band through their pre-performance ritual. 'Tonight!' they chant, 'The Diamond Club! You burn!'

As they head out for the stage, the Jeff Healey Band know that they won't need special powers to win over this audience. Canada's hottest new band, a three-piece led by the young, white blind guitarist who has been hailed as 'the best since Eric Clapton', are back on home turf. They've taken time off from a major American tour to return to Toronto to appear live on television at the Juno Awards (the Canadian version of the

Grammys), and now, as Healey explains to his audience, 'we felt we'd come down and make a little noise. Welcome to the party.'

He's perched on a chair at the front of a stage that overlooks a dance floor packed with nearly 1000 followers who know that they might not get too many opportunities to see Healey in a setting like this again, now he's become a celebrity in America and Europe. He's special not just because he's reviving sixties-style blues-influenced guitar rock, but because he really has taken over where Clapton and Jeff Beck left off, pushing the blues/rock guitar style into new areas. Texan bluesman Stevie Ray Vaughan, who was partly instrumental

(Opposite) Howlin' Wolf

in discovering Healey, claimed that 'Jeff's going to revolutionise the way the guitar can be played.' Even B. B. King, the best-known and best-loved surviving bluesman of them all, had been enthusing about Healey when I'd met him back in London earlier. 'His guitar style is different – he's one of a kind.'

The good-looking blond boy onstage was showing the home-town crowd why he deserved such attention. His guitar was tuned in the normal way, but he held it in his lap, with his left hand pressing down on the strings from above, rather than holding it round the neck in the usual way. It looked bizarre, but the results were spectacular. He was obviously using all five left-hand fingers for vibrato effects, and stretching out with his left thumb to reach chord patterns that could never be attempted by a conventional guitarist.

The songs were pretty unconventional, too – at least judged alongside the synth-pop and white soul that makes up so much modern music. He started off with an upbeat ballad of his own, 'My Little Girl', that developed into a rippling, then pounding improvisation, before moving onto a version of John Hiatt's 'Confidence Man', a gentle ballad, and then heading back to the sixties for a powerful and wailing treatment of the old Cream hit from twenty years earlier, 'White Room', and the Doors' R&B favourite, 'Roadhouse Blues'. 'We're talking about determination here,' said the blind guitar hero, as he first persuaded the audience to join him in singing 'I woke up this morning and got myself a beer', and then got up from his chair to play the guitar behind his head, and then with his teeth, while never letting up on the fluid, wailing attack.

This may not be the blues as it was played in Mississippi in the twenties and thirties, Memphis and Chicago in the forties, fifties and sixties, or in London in the sixties (though that's a lot closer), but the influences are still there in this latest white hybrid version of a style that has been one of the cornerstones of American popular music and rock'n'roll. Healey may owe his success, in part,

to the enthusiasm of famous bluesmen for his playing, but he doesn't see himself as a blues musician in any classic tradition. As he explains backstage, 'I'm not a traditionalist at all. I'm not actually a blues player. I have some leanings that way – a blues direction. It has the influence.'

What is more, he started out playing the clubs in one of those North American cities where the blues has never died. Toronto may not have the blues tradition of Chicago or Texas, but the white guitar bands of Canada have listened intently to the great black heroes from south of the border. When he appeared at the Juno Awards, Healey was playing to an audience that included Robbie Robertson, now a successful soloist but once a member of local roadhouse heroes Ronnie Hawkins and the Hawks, and later that most highly respected outfit, The Band, whose early playing was heavily influenced by bluesmen like Howlin' Wolf. In the seventies and eighties the Canadian blues was kept alive by local heroes like The Downchild Blues Band, and by dozens of part-time enthusiasts playing in bars and tiny clubs.

The Jeff Healey Band headed off for one of those clubs once their show at The Diamond was over. Chicago's diner is on Queen Street West, an area of bars, markets and restaurants halfway between the towering downtown skyscrapers and the city's university. It is an area where it seems only appropriate that a record store should sell old Ronnie Hawkins albums or act as headquarters for the Toronto Blues Society, and that two former colleagues of Robbie Robertson in The Band, Rick Danko and Garth Hudson, should be discovered playing in a music bar where a sign announced 'Dress code in effect – postively no polyester leisure suits after 10pm'.

It was well after that hour by now, and Chicago's was packed. Downstairs the music hadn't yet started, but upstairs in a small cramped room known rather incongruously as Checkerboard West, there was a blues jam already in session. The house band, led by a bearded harmonica player, somehow managed to keep playing despite the fact

(Above) Jeff Healey and (opposite) Texan bluesman Stevie Ray Vaughan, partly responsible for discovering Jeff Healey

that a crowd of maybe 100 were squashed all around them. It was here that the Jeff Healey Band had started out three years earlier, playing both upstairs and downstairs and 'working up our act'.

Healey was keen to play back here tonight, and space was found for his chair, while his bass-player Joe Rockman and drummer Tom Stephen edged in behind. Someone suggested a Big Bill Broonzy tune, then an up-tempo boogie, and Healey began to rock up the blues, with a delighted audience squeezed in around him, watching his left-hand technique in astonishment. It had become a night to remember.

Healey is still only twenty-two, but has already, as Tom Stephen put it, been 'influenced by the spirit of the blues' and has tried 'to carry it even further', just like Cream or the early Fleetwood Mac had done in the sixties. Healey had first heard the music in clubs, or 'through radio, and through friends', and had decided 'it seemed to be the most comfortable style of performing, for myself. It seemed easiest to communicate with an audience that way.'

The world's latest guitar hero is soft-spoken, has a gently wicked sense of humour, and is deceptively tough. In an evening spent travelling around the Toronto clubs, and discussing his history, he never once mentioned his blindness, or suggested that it had been in any way a disability. Even so, it was his blindness (caused by an eye cancer at the age of one) that led indirectly to his unique style. He was given his first guitar at the age of three when, he says:

> I was a pretty normal kid except I had this obsession for incoherent musical sounds. I might have discovered a few new chords in those days, and started playing it like a lap steel guitar, tuned to a chord and played with a steel bar in the left hand. Then at four, five or six I learned standard tuning and started working out all the chords, but still holding the guitar the same way I did with the slide – on my lap. Then I threw away the slide and began putting my hand on the top of the neck, and working out the chords that way. And here we are!

It wasn't quite as easy as that, of course. Healey was sent to blind school in Ontario, where the curriculum included piano lessons 'and I found

them extremely boring. I liked playing piano, but what I wanted to play, not what was being taught.' He was an academic success, but when he moved onto high school 'I found I had to work, and I hated that.' So he quit, and managed to get a place in a local music college 'but hated that as much as I hated high school'. He left after an academic dispute with a music history teacher (Healey still maintains that he was in the right).

By now, he admits, he 'wasn't very popular around the family' but decided to 'turn all the time and energy I had into playing and trying to get something working'. He formed his first group, Blue Direction, when he was in his mid-teens, and now spent all his time 'working little pick-up jobs with different bands, filling in for other guitar players', on one occasion even sitting in with a reggae band.

'I spent about a year at it, going absolutely nowhere,' says Healey. 'I was even thinking about going back to school or into broadcasting.' But then, in classic showbiz tradition, he got his break. A friend asked him to go to a local Toronto club to see Albert Collins, the Texan-born blues guitarist whose upbeat, amplified style was once promoted by Canned Heat, who had helped make him a popular figure with the white hippy audiences on the West Coast in the sixties. Healey was introduced to Collins, 'and we got talking about how I held the guitar'. Collins was intrigued, asked the then nineteen-year-old to get up and play with his band, and was so impressed that he asked if Healey could come back at the end of the week, and sit in with him and fellow Texan bluesman Stevie Ray Vaughan (whose brother Jimmie plays with that classic R&B outfit, The Fabulous Thunderbirds).

It was these veteran bluesmen who first appreciated Healey's talent, 'and I couldn't believe what I heard. I couldn't believe it until it happened. But I went down and did it, and it was a big media event – a lot of people wanted to see Stevie Ray turn up at a small club.'

After that night at Albert's Hall, a Toronto venue that specialises in folk and blues, Healey knew he had his chance to 'either put up or shut up. Nobody had heard of me, except when I'd shown up at jam sessions, and the bar owners had wanted nothing to do with me before that. So I

(Above) Robert Cray – the most successful of the new blues artists and (opposite) Mississippi bluesman Son House, 'rediscovered' by British blues enthusiasts in the late sixties

had to get a serious band together.'

It was now that Healey showed how tough he could be. He got together with Joe and Tom (who also took on the role of manager), and they toured across the bars and clubs of Canada, playing 'whatever we knew, collectively' and sometimes giving three-hour-long shows a night as they built up their following. Next, they wanted a record deal, but this wasn't easy in a country where, as Tom puts it, the companies are 'programmed by the Americans and won't do anything for their own. One A&R man even told me that we needed a gimmick – and here we were with this good-looking blond kid who plays guitar better than you've ever seen!'

They made it eventually, by starting their own label, Forte, making their own video, and then sending Tom down to New York to hustle the American labels. He secured a deal with Arista's legendary boss Clive Davis, who in his years with CBS had signed everyone from Janis Joplin to Edgar Winter. When the full band interrupted their hectic touring to fly down for their first meeting with Davis 'in a skyscraper office with a desk bigger than three of these rooms', Tom says he was 'scared shitless', but Healey fell sound asleep.

They took much the same approach when asked to appear in a major Hollywood movie, before they'd even recorded their first album. *Roadhouse*, which stars Patrick Swayze (best known for *Dirty Dancing*) had a role for a blues/rock band with a blind guitarist who plays on his lap. There aren't too many like that around, so it was no surprise to learn that the scriptwriter had once seen Healey perform. The band were crucial for the film, but the film-makers treated them for what they were – a bunch of unknowns who had come straight from the Canadian bar circuit. They only secured the film deal that they wanted after threatening to quit on several occasions, and they were only allowed to perform the theme song, The Doors' 'Roadhouse Blues', after a personal vetting from former Doors keyboard player Ray Manzarek.

At first, he hadn't liked the idea of some unknown band playing the song, and had refused permission, but was eventually persuaded to come up to the studio at least to hear the Healey version. 'Everyone was sweating,' said Tom, 'because it was so important for the film.' Needless to say, Manzarek loved it – and so did all the other stars in town. Tom Petty, Bob Seger, Mark Knopfler, Neil Young and Stevie Wonder all came to check out the new blind white boy reviving a sixties-style power trio, and the blues.

Healey may have been the latest blues-rocker to make the big time, but he didn't have the field to himself. The eighties had already produced one brand-new blues superstar, who had won himself gold albums and a world-wide following. This was a cool and good-looking black singer, songwriter and guitarist who had come up the hard way, scuffling around the bars and clubs of the world for fifteen years as he proved that an updated but instantly recognisable reworking of the blues could still sound absolutely right in the new CD market.

Robert Cray updated the blues traditions of anguish and pain (and immaculate guitar work), as opposed to Healey's boisterous bar-room style, but the two of them had something in common. Both started out in parts of North America that can hardly be described as classic blues territory (Cray formed his own band not in Texas, Memphis or Chicago but up in Oregon on the northwest Pacific coast), and both had been inspired and helped by Albert Collins. Cray first decided that he wanted to play the blues when he heard Collins performing at an outdoor festival back in 1969 (and then again at his own high school graduation two years later), and so it was only appropriate that he should become part of the Texan guitar hero's West Coast touring band later in the seventies.

Born in Georgia in 1955, Cray spent his childhood travelling, across America and to West Germany, as his family followed his serviceman father to different postings. The young Robert Cray had heard folk, blues and rock on the radio, and after hearing Collins he formed his band up in Oregon, and here he first joined up with his bass-playing partner and stage clown Richard Cousins. The band had listened to veteran bluesmen like Howlin' Wolf and Muddy Waters, to soul singers like Sam Cooke, and to white blues-rock heroes like Eric Clapton. The influences gradually came together as they played around the northwest blues circuit, and then (when not backing Collins) they gradually expanded their range and their following, as they began to notch up around 200 shows a year.

Amidst the almost constant touring, the Robert Cray band began recording. The first album *Who's Been Talking* was released on the now defunct indie label, Tomato, and had already been 'in the can' for two years when it appeared in 1980. It was followed by *Bad Influence*, and the 1985 set

False Accusations, which was the first to appear in *Billboard*'s album charts. The following year Cray was back in the best-sellers with *Showdown*, on which he was reunited with his hero Albert Collins, along with bluesman Johnny Copeland. This time he earned a Grammy as well.

By now it was inevitable that Cray would be signed to a major label and would start to play the concert hall circuit instead of clubs. He didn't just become a new blues success, he became a minor sensation. His first album for Mercury, *Strong Persuader*, sold over 1 000 000 in America alone, and 'went platinum' (as it also did in Australia, New Zealand, and Holland; in Britain it merely 'went gold'). The 1988 follow-up, *Don't Be Afraid Of The Dark*, brought another batch of awards, as the band continued to run round and round the globe playing to their new followers.

So how had he done it? Partly by a mix of styles, with a touch of R&B and rock, or the soul styles of Motown and Stax (echoed by the inclusion of the Memphis Horns on his hit albums), added in with the blues. Partly because of his light, fluid, emotional, economic and never indulgent guitar work, and his cool, neat vocals (matching his cool, neat good looks). And partly because the songs (which are written by Cray, his band, and their producers Bruce Bromberg and Dennis Walker) manage to update all those old blues stories of woman trouble and hard times, and add in a nasty element for the eighties, the blues *noir*. Cray sings about cheating, voyeurism, blackmail, betrayal, guilt, and being given a hard time in return. He likes blues to deal with 'real-life stories and situations', which means that he includes songs about down-and-outs, or a woman who stole his credit cards. This is no archive music from the past, but a mixture of blues and rock that sounds like contemporary city music fit for New York, London or even Tokyo (where Cray, and the blues in general, have a particularly large following).

Cray and Healey have done more than make their names by reviving and updating the style that's at the heart of much of the Western popular music of the twentieth century. The blues may be the music that's influenced and inspired much folk music, jazz, gospel and rock'n'roll, but for a long time it had seemed like a slowly dying genre. The old masters, who had started out in Mississippi,

(Above) John Lee Hooker and (opposite) Muddy Waters – Chicago bluesman

Memphis or Chicago in the twenties, thirties and forties were dwindling, and even the white folk and rock enthisiasts who had learned from them (often enjoying far greater commercial success than their mentors) were moving on.

Pomp, theatrics and synthesized white soul led to an inevitable backlash. By the mid-eighties, many white audiences were searching for 'authenticity' or 'honesty' in their pop music, just as those in the folk revival of the late fifties had done. This somewhat romantic and idealised search had led to young enthusiasts scouring the American South to rediscover acoustic bluesmen who had played a role in the early days, when the Mississippi Delta blues, the Texan country blues, the Eastern Seaboard blues, or the 'holy blues' of the singing street preachers, had all evolved from the collision of the field hollers of the slaves with European folk styles.

The young white enthusiasts of the late fifties and early sixties had been remarkably successful, much to the astonishment of a whole set of venerable musicians who never guessed that they'd suddenly be treated as celebrities and invited to play at the Newport Folk Festival or tour round Europe in 'blues packages'. Sleepy John Estes (who went on to influence the likes of Ry Cooder) was 'rediscovered' in Texas, as was the great Lightnin' Hopkins, who'd given up hopes of commercial success and gone back to street singing. Bukka White was tracked down by John Fahey; Mississippi Fred McDowell was invited to make his first recording at the age of fifty-five (and later to tour with Bonnie Raitt); while Mississippi John Hurt (who until now was known to blues fans for recordings he'd made back in 1928) suddenly discovered, at the age of seventy-one, that he was being praised for his complex guitar work and erotic love songs like 'Salty Dog'.

Through singers like these, or the wonderful team of Sonny Terry and Brownie McGhee, the white audiences of the sixties learned the history of the blues and a great deal that they didn't know about the history of their own country. Blues had survived partly because it was so versatile –

anyone could learn to play the three guitar chords, and sing the two repeated phrases and answering line that constitute a straightforward delta blues. But that simple form was the basis for emotional, subtle, or sophisticated variation: from the classic early blues songs of hard times, loneliness and troubled relationships, through to displays of elaborate guitar technique, or the piano-based dance styles that developed in Texas or Louisiana.

In the thirties and forties, when black Americans migrated up the Mississippi to find work in Memphis, Chicago or Detroit, they took the blues with them, and the music inevitably changed in the process. The likes of John Lee Hooker, Howlin' Wolf and Muddy Waters developed a harder, amplified guitar style, while B. B. King – who would become the best-loved and best-known bluesman of them all – incorporated jazz techniques into his fluid and massively influential lead guitar work. The amplified blues players of the forties led in turn to the R&B dance bands that became the biggest influence of all on the new black/white fusion music of the fifties, rock'n'roll.

The start of the rock era had an odd effect on the blues. Established performers like Howlin' Wolf, Muddy Waters and B. B. King just kept going, while other lesser-known bluesmen found they were out of favour in the fast-changing musical climate. But then along came folk revival, and the acoustic, country blues performers found they were back in favour. Once this was over, in the mid-sixties, the amplified blues players and black R&B stars found they were courted by the new 'progressive' rock bands. Rock was moving on, and blues provided an excellent starting point. White American bands from Canned Heat to ZZ Top, and even The Doors and the Grateful Dead, all made use of blues styles, while in Britain the new white blues scene led to the emergence of guitar heroes like Eric Clapton and Jeff Beck, and blues-based bands like the (early) Fleetwood Mac and The Rolling Stones.

It was only right that The Stones should take B. B. King on tour with them in 1968 at the height

115

of their fame, and he at least, certainly didn't resent the fact that young white foreigners were doing so well with the music. Sitting in a London hotel room twenty-one years later he claimed that 'the doors weren't open to the blues until the rock era and we had people like Eric Clapton who spoke out for it. It opened the doors to an audience I hadn't been used to.'

By the late sixties, the blues boom was at its height, but it didn't last. 'Progressive' rock bands used the versatile style as a basis for anything from psychedelic improvisation to heavy metal, but throughout the seventies and early eighties, pop music gradually drifted away from the power and passion of its blues roots. Black musical fashion had moved on, to soul, reggae or rap, and though there was always an audience for the likes of B. B. King, the blues was becoming marginalised. Many of the legendary performers were no longer at work (Howlin' Wolf died in 1976 and Muddy Waters in 1983) and though there was a new generation of players like Buddy Guy, Edgar and Johnny Winter, Stevie Ray Vaughan or Johnny Copeland, it seemed that the great days of the blues were over.

Then in the late eighties the blues scene changed once again. Robert Cray and Jeff Healey emerged as the new heroes, and their success was an indication of a wider change in pop fashion – a change that had been reflected by the personal experiences and enthusiasms of the most successful rock band of the eighties, U2.

Like many pop audiences around the world, U2 learned about the blues after other musicians had advised them to look back at the history of popular music, and the 'roots' styles that had come before rock'n'roll. Bob Dylan enthused to them about Irish folk music (which he knew more about than the Dublin band did), while Peter Wolf of The J. Geils Band, and The Rolling Stones' Mick Jagger and Keith Richards told them about the roots of American pop, about country music – and the blues. It was after listening to records by the likes of Robert Johnson and John Lee Hooker, and realising that the best blues could mix raw power and emotion as well as any rock style, that Bono wrote the blues-influenced 'Silver And Gold', which appeared on the *Sun City* album.

After being introduced to the blues by The Rolling Stones, U2 did just what The Rolling Stones had done in the sixties – they got together with B. B. King. They visited him backstage after he had given a concert in Dublin, and it was here, according to King, that 'I mentioned to Bono that I'd like to get him to write a song'. The result was the U2/King collaboration 'When Love Comes To Town', as heard and seen on the *Rattle And Hum* album and film. It's ironic that King should be 'very very nervous' at appearing with U2, but he was pleased with the result. For one thing, the sixty-three-year-old blues legend noted that he had once again won a brand-new, young audience. Next, he said, he wanted his record sales to equal those of the blues newcomers Robert Cray and Jeff Healey.

'Both are great artists, and they're doing some beautiful stuff, and we need it,' said King, before adding an unexpected comment that showed that the veteran bluesman wasn't totally happy that the new boys were getting such attention.

It seems to me that if you're Mike Tyson, everyone wants you to get your pants dusted once in a while, and it's the same with B. B. King, that's been around for a long time. They always want the new kid on the block to bloody my nose a bit.

A few hours later, he was onstage at London's Hammersmith Odeon before a packed and delighted crowd, showing that a veteran could still leave the very best of the new boys standing, at least when it came to a live show (his latest album, which aims for the commercial mainstream, is a disappointment in comparison). A genial, bulky figure, he proved that he's still in fine voice, and can still play quite unbelievably fluid and emotional solos, gently coaxing his black Gibson guitar Lucille (the fifteenth Lucille he's used since the fifties), with his left hand quivering as he produces the vibrato effects that are part of his trademark. He sang blues laments and songs of love affairs gone wrong, like his hit from nearly twenty years ago, 'The Thrill Is Gone', with Lucille almost literally crying back at him, then switched to good-time, up-tempo rolling blues and songs that showed off his sense of humour and fun. The blues can do all this, in the hands of a true master, and that's why the music has survived and changed, to be rediscovered by a new generation.

(*Background*) *B. B. King on the road and* (*opposite bottom*) *The Rolling Stones, circa mid-sixties*

Robert Cray and Jeff Healey have worked wonders in making sure that the blues, or blues-rock, remains at the heart of much great popular music. But even the best new blues has some way to go before it can match the work of a truly legendary survivor like B. B. King.

INTO THE HOT-

EXOTICA AND WORLD MUSIC FUSIONS

DAVID TOOP

It was 1860. Count Eulenberg, the first ambassador of Prussia in Japan, took office in a style that hinted, with blind premonition, at world events to follow. Eulenberg marched forty marines behind a military brass band from the Yokohama pier to his new home in Akabane. According to Eta Harich-Schneider, the author of *A History of Japanese Music*, 'the Edo people were stunned'.

Six years later, the *daimyo* of Fukui petitioned the French embassy to appoint a French officer to teach French military music to the band in his private army and by 1874, following a suggestion from the Japanese Emperor, there were moves to include Western music in the repertoire of the gakunin, the musicians who played Japan's ancient gagaku court music. The reasoning behind this faltering step towards a fusion of East/West pomposity and nationalism lies in a report drawn up after ministry consultation. It said:

> We have repeatedly adopted music from other countries. This was a natural human development. Now the situation is the same with respect to European music. Not only in the army and navy, but also at court ceremonies and banquets we need the music of the West.[1]

In 1889, at the Paris Exposition Universelle, Claude Debussy made a personal discovery which

we now take as a universal, albeit arguable, fact. Already sympathetic and alert to the exotic in art and literature, his exposure to music from Java, Cambodia, Japan and Vietnam caused him to realign the relative values of Western and non-Western music. He perceived qualities in Javanese music, which, for him, overshadowed aspects of acknowledged European masters. 'Javanese music is based on a type of counterpoint,' he wrote, 'by comparison with which that of Palestrina pales.'

A direct influence of Javanese music and Vietnamese dance-drama on Debussy's own writing for piano or his lyrical drama *Pélleas et Mélisande* is elusive, certainly harder to pin down than the Spanish influence in *Preludes* and *Estampes*. Perhaps the music he heard was largely an affirmation of his own exotic, impressionistic tendencies. His example, however, was significant. A major European composer had suggested that the European tradition was not inviolate, not unsurpassable, not the apex of human achievement.

Debussy was not the only Frenchman to be impressed by a Parisian exhibition. At the Exposition Ethnographique de l'Afrique Occidentale in 1895, a physician named Felix-Louis Regnault filmed a Wolof woman making pots. This was, effectively, the first ethnographic film, followed at the beginning of this century by Baldwin Spencer's footage of Australian Aboriginal ceremonies, Rudolph Puch's attempts to film in Papua New Guinea and Southwest Africa, as well as various exotic novelties, ethno-bites perhaps, made by fledgling film companies of the period, shot among Pueblo Indians or Samoan circus dancers and offered as tasters to the hungry new movie audiences of the world.

A few years later, Star Film, the company owned by cinema visionary Georges Melies, attempted financial recuperation in a period of difficulties by filming melodramas in Tahiti and New Zealand. Melies' brother, Gaston, directed a number of these films, including the intriguing-sounding *Loved By A Maori Chieftainess*, but

South Seas humidity destroyed many of them, perhaps in anticipatory revenge for a future of fashion shoots and adventure films set in exotic locations.[2]

According to Walter Benjamin, writing on nineteenth-century expositions, 'They open up a phantasmagoria that people enter to be amused.'[3] This amusement, the search, the embrace, the intoxication of the exotic is one of the major shaping forces of the past 100 years. The word 'exotic' has the sense of an alien froth, a titillatory otherness, a newness which throws the old into doubt, clouds the familiar or displaces it for a short time or forever. The exotic implies something poorly understood, an invasion of sensation too seductive to resist. Most of all, the exotic creates, in Umberto Eco's neologism, a hyper-reality, a world that seems more real, more potent, than reality. In this sense, from the close of the nineteenth century up until the present and with a growing frenzy, we live in an imagined future of exotic blends, fusions, exchanges, thefts, infusions and dreamworlds.

In *A Theory of Expositions*, Umberto Eco wrote:

It was only with the expositions of the nineteenth century that the marvels of the year 2000 began to be announced. And it is only with Disneyland and Disney World that concern with the Space Age is combined with nostalgia for a fairytale past.[4]

Perhaps Disneyland is an echo of those Japanese efforts to forge a future from the intractable elements of gagaku, a fairytale past of their own, harking back to the Heiau period of the ninth to eleventh centuries, and the equally stern yet altogether more modern, brash, exotic and literally forward-marching militarism of the brass band. In Japan, these were the beginnings of a romance with Western music which offered the privileged classes an opportunity to leave their own country and experience the exotic glamour of Europe.

Exotica is relative. Everybody has seen photographs of dancers from the Highlands of Papua

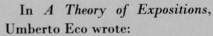

(*Above*) *Karlheinz Stockhausen and* (*opposite*) *Madonna – a true 'world music' superstar?*

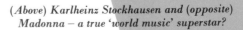

New Guinea, decorated with Bird of Paradise plumes, fragments of mirrors, sunglasses, bottle tops and white nylon bras. These pictures are seen as amusing or quaint, yet what real difference is there between such combinations of the commonplace and the strange and the display of exotic pre-cooked meals – such as Moules Bonne Femme, Seafood Tagliatelle and Chinese-Style Chicken – a few feet away from the white nylon bras in Marks & Spencer?

In *Exotica*, a book of works by the contemporary Japanese illustrator Yosuke Kawamura, the exotic exchange is either consciously realised through drawings of American GIs with their Japanese lovers – Kimiko and Bobby, Nancy and Kenzo, Steve and Sachiko – and fantasies of a samurai resting by a Coca-Cola machine, or it is shown as a seductive otherness, a near obsessive depiction of Latin American salsa stars – Tito Rodriguez, Nicky Marrero, Ismael Miranda, Hector Lavoe and, going further back to Cuba and a deeper more distant exotica, Arsenio Rodriguez Y Su Conjunto.

Certain places, such as Cuba, Japan, Brazil, Morocco, America, India, China, Bali and Jamaica, encapsulate exotic myths and every country has its own Shangri-La. Musically speaking, as with anything else, fashions change. Chinoiserie and 'Turkish' themes coloured music in the eighteenth century but the history of exotic music and cultural exchange is also the history of colonialism and slavery. In the context of European colonial expansion into Africa and Asia during the nineteenth century, the music of both coloniser and colonised was bound to be irrevocably changed by contact and the lure of the exotic.

'The yearning for the exotic is the subconscious mourning for what has been destroyed,' wrote Ramon Pelinski, 'and at the same time the justification for colonial expansion.'[5] Just as industry created an insatiable demand for overseas resources, so the technological revolutions in travel and communications – the steamship, the steam railway, the telegraph – allowed for transportation, freedom of movement, marketing and plunder.

This relatively easy access allowed more enlightened travellers to realise, in panic, that their arrival was equivalent to allowing air to enter a

sealed tomb. The supposed primeval cultures they encountered would begin to disintegrate and fade away in their presence. Luckily or disastrously, the railways and steamships that had transported them into the beyond could transport musicians back to Europe to perform. The invention of film enabled visual documentation of vanishing societies to begin, and later, the development of magnetic audio tape began in earnest the process of capturing music for study and posterity.

If there was an urgency in all this recording then there was also an enticing danger. The exotic carried with it the myth of reversion back into primitivism, dark forces unleashed, and the sort of atavism only courted by occultists. In *Heart of Darkness*, Joseph Conrad wrote:

They howled and leaped, and spun, and made horrid faces; but what thrilled you was just the thought of their humanity – like yours – the thought of your remote kinship with this wild and passionate uproar. Ugly. Yes, it was ugly enough; but if you were man enough you would admit to yourself that there was in you the faintest trace of a response to the terrible frankness of that noise, a dim suspicion of there being a meaning in it which you – you so remote from the night of first ages – could comprehend.

Some decades later, films like *King Kong*, *Mighty Joe Young* and *Tarzan The Ape Man* provided a metaphor for the philosophy that you can take the boy/ape/ape-man out of the jungle but you can't take the jungle out of the boy. The jungle drums that drove white men mad, or the strange oriental tones heard in opium dens; these were ideas held by repressed, fearful, tightly

wrapped people, the defenders of civilisation against musical miscegenation.

Some travellers, even those with an interest in recording native music, have tended to use their recording equipment to promote the cause of Western music and perhaps break this threatening spell. During an expedition along the Orinoco and Amazon rivers in 1950, Alain Gheerbrant and his companions played a Mozart record to Maquiritari Indians. Gheerbrant wrote:

> I do not know if music is really the universal language people often say it is, but I shall never forget that it was the music of Mozart to which we owed our rare moments when the chasm which centuries of evolution had dug between us, civilised white men of the twentieth century, and them, the barbarians of the Stone Age, was almost completely bridged.[6]

First curiosity and fascination, then scholarly documentation and conservation, then absorption in alien musics and finally the attempts to fuse diverse strands of musical tradition. This bridging of the cultural gap has been the central notion of fusions in world music.

There is a contradiction in world music fusions between a desire for a future of human understanding (a millennial unity) and the historical background of colonialism, slavery and war. Even the tools of conserving disappearing musics came from war; the accelerated development of both magnetic tape and disc recording during the Second World War and the dramatic advances in portable recording and playback technology by Sony, surrounded by the post-war devastation of bombing in southern Tokyo.

It was a pre-electronic method of documentation, a by-product of the genocidal impulses that characterised the creation of modern America, that led to England's first public display of non-European music from America. In the early eighteen-forties, according to ethnomusicologist Klaus Wachsmann,

> George Catlin, the American painter of Indian life, maintained for several years an exhibition of his paintings at which groups of Ojibwa and later Iowa Indians performed regularly, mainly as a publicity stunt; the Indians also put on shows at Vauxhall Gardens and at a command performance before Queen Victoria. Later they went to the Continent.[7]

When Walter Benjamin said of nineteenth-century expositions, 'they open up a phantasmagoria that people enter to be amused,' he also wrote, 'The entertainment industry facilitates this by elevating people to the level of commodities.' World music, along with its 'performers', has become a commodity, like any other. In 1935, anthropologist Kilton Stewart, writing his paper *Dream Theory In Malaya*, could not have known that his study of the dream-telling and singing of the aboriginal Senoi of Malaya would become a building brick in the music and ideas of Jon Hassell. Hassell is an American composer and performer whose music aims at what he describes as 'Fourth World', a utopia that has been described as 'a unified primitive/futuristic sound combining features of world ethnic styles with advanced electronic techniques'.[8] Hassell's music is perhaps one of the most successful attempts at this recurrent ideal, a smoking throbbing pulse full of indefinable exotic allusions. His own progress as a recording artist and theorist is a virtual role model: a period of study with Karlheinz Stockhausen; performing with Terry Riley and LaMonte Young; a student of Classical Indian vocal music with Pandit Pran Nath; a composer/performer of semi-improvised music embracing computer and digital innovations in music technology; a sampler of 'exotic' recordings, and a collaborator with musicians from varying traditions and ethnic backgrounds. Additionally, it should be said that his records have been marketed as a marginal kind of popular music.

Hassell has described his work as a 'proposal for a "coffee coloured" classical music for the future'.[9] This precursor of the more insulting critical term, 'beige music', a description of music which shares the gestures of black soul and funk and white rock to a degree which dilutes the force of both. This is a nagging doubt for many theorists and exponents of world music. Is world music an internationalist blurring of differentiation, a descent into a global soup of no distinct flavour?

Some writers have deplored the implications of musical internationalism yet also warned against provincial regionalism, a necessary scholarly equivocation which is brutally swept aside by a

(Background and opposite) Duke Ellington

tide of seductive images and role models in the shape of Madonna, Michael Jackson, Sting or Tina Turner. For Stockhausen, one of the pioneers of the concept of 'world music', particularly in his tape work from 1966 *Telemusik*, 'Every person has all of mankind within himself.'[10] In his notes on *Telemusik*, an electronic transformation of fragments of recorded music from Africa, the Amazon, Hungary, China, Spain, Vietnam, Bali and Japan, Stockhausen wrote, 'I wanted to come closer to an old, an ever-recurrent dream: to go a step forward towards writing, not 'my' music, but a music of the whole world, of all lands and races.'[11]

In the sixties this was becoming a common vision, manifested partly as a convergence of musical initiatives which had been developing over the previous seven decades, as well as by other slowly ripening interests in exotic arts and rites, philosophies and religions, drugs and dress. Thanks to global wars, revolutions, great economic migrations, refugee movements, the rapacious progress of industry, religious mission work, tourism, radio, television, cinema, the gramophone record, the telephone, the car and the aeroplane – all in this century – the gradual collapse of European empires abroad had no effect on the numerous cultural borrowings and exchanges that began with the march of the Prussian ambassador into Japan and Debussy's stroll around a Paris exposition.

The variety of influences on musical development in the twentieth century is dazzlingly complex. Experiments in new and exotic forms were, and still are, often flawed with contradiction. Richard Wagner was absorbed by Buddhist and Hindu ideas at the same time as having an enthusiasm for the German-Aryan master race theories of Houston Stewart Chamberlain, his son-in-law, and the diplomat and orientalist Arthur de Gobineau. Puccini's opera *Madame Butterfly*, was based on Pierre Loti's racist book, *Madame Chrysantheme*. And works like Rimsky-Korsakov's *Scheherazade*, enthralling and influential though they were, were ancestors of a strain of exoticism found in *Emmanuelle* films, travelogues, kitsch 'international cuisine' restaurants and, at its most extreme, the Florida Disney World 'World Showcase'.

The influence of folk musics and alien philosophies has been among the prime elements, however, in the relentless redefinition of musical language during the last 100 years. Béla Bartók, Igor Stravinsky, Charles Ives, Vaughan Williams, Lou Harrison, Ruth Crawford Seeger, Colin McPhee, John Cage, Karlheinz Stockhausen, Pierre Boulez and Harry Partch, to name but a few, were all composers, many of them American, who consciously enriched or disrupted the European tradition out of which their music grew.

Outside Europe and America, composers like Toru Takemitsu, Maki Ishii and Minoru Miki from Japan, Hector Villa-Lobos from Brazil, José Maceda from the Philippines, Chou Wen-Chung from China, Isang Yun from Korea and Peter Sculthorpe from Australia, among many other composers from all over the globe, are engaged in the same process, sometimes abandoning a slavish devotion to imitations of European music for a rediscovery of their own musical traditions and an attempt to create a new union from the two. The fastest creations of new musical alloys and hybrids have happened in rather less formal spheres. There has been nothing to equal the dramatic impact of blues, jazz and R&B in the twentieth century, for example, and many of these composers were as deeply impressed by jazz as by Zen Buddhism, Balinese gamelan or the folk songs of Hungary.

Their conceptual framework left otherwise radical composers like Cage and Stockhausen unable to embrace either the improvisational foundation of jazz or its extremely broad appeal, an appeal which could offer complete intellectual and emotional satisfaction in music played in a bar full of drunks, or that could frame improvisational brilliance within the themes and chords of a popular song. A number of jazz musicians, including the Modern Jazz Quartet and Ornette Coleman, strove to break this link between jazz and the noisy, smoky clubs that operated on the fringes of crime and the sex industry, seeing this environment as an 'exotic' element of the music that only provided atmosphere and context for those listeners who saw jazz in a naive racist light, as a savage, sexual, dark music.

Arising as they did in America, blues, jazz and R&B would clearly not have been so exotic were it not for racial discrimination. To cloud the issue further, jazz composers themselves drew on exotic themes. One of the greatest periods of Duke Elling-

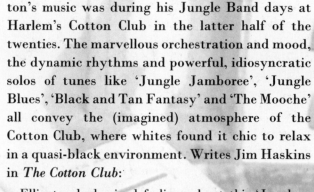

ton's music was during his Jungle Band days at Harlem's Cotton Club in the latter half of the twenties. The marvellous orchestration and mood, the dynamic rhythms and powerful, idiosyncratic solos of tunes like 'Jungle Jamboree', 'Jungle Blues', 'Black and Tan Fantasy' and 'The Mooche' all convey the (imagined) atmosphere of the Cotton Club, where whites found it chic to relax in a quasi-black environment. Writes Jim Haskins in *The Cotton Club*:

> Ellington had mixed feelings about this 'Jungle Band' reputation. He was not simply catering to white tastes. 'As a student of Negro history I had, in any case, a natural inclination in this direction,' he would later say.

In 1950, travelling among Moi tribespeople in Vietnam, Norman Lewis observed during his reception in a village longhouse, that:

> On the beams, hung with leather shields, crossbows and drinking horns, were the art treasures I was coming to expect; a daringly sporting Vietnamese calendar showing a bathing beauty, a car-chassis oiling chart, a Tarzan cartoon.[12]

In the present, should you travel to a small town in Algeria called Tlemcen, you will find a recording studio full of the sound of Algerian rai music, drum machines, electric guitars, analog keyboards, Arabic percussion, and digital samples of Japanese shakuhachi flutes. In the space between the double sheets of glass that separate the control room from the live room of the studio there is an Indian sitar, trapped like a sleeping peacock in a zoo. Purely ornamental, perhaps nostalgic, it is a reminder of the complex way in which music intersects, running in crazy lines from one outpost to the next and mating frantically as it goes, abandoning offspring, and creating prodigies and monsters.

Towards the end of the sixties, the owner of the sitar, producer Rachid Baba, was influenced by The Beatles and The Rolling Stones. They, in their turn, were both being temporarily influenced by music from India and the global electronic montages that had followed in the wake of Stockhausen's *Telemusik*, Richard Maxfield's *Bacchanale* and John Cage's *Variations IV*.

Rachid wanted to play Beatles and Rolling Stones music but not like the insipid Western pop cover-versions that were threatening to sweep aside indigenous Algerian music; consequently he formed a group to perform 'English' rock in Arabic. Some of this hybrid English/Afro-American/Algerian music was dressed up with the sitar lead lines that were a hallmark of so-called raga rock and the psychedelic era of 1966–68.

Other notable world musicians were similarly impressed by this phase of popular music. For example, Djavan, in Brazil, sang in a group somewhat scandalously named LSD, specialising solely in covers of Beatles songs. Djavan was slightly too young to be a part of the Tropicalista movement in Brazil but those who were at its forefront and also alert to the new European and American popular music – Gilberto Gil, Chico Buarque, Gal Costa, Milton Nascimento and others – saw no contradiction in using this music as part of a movement which celebrated the African and Amazonian roots of Brazilian culture. This simultaneous back-and-forth, *retronuevo* avant-gardism, is typical of world music fusions, in its desire for roots and tradition while creating new and unfamiliar hybrids. Musicians like Rachid and Djavan are conscious that all types of modern music are international hybrids but their leanings toward the undifferentiated 'world soup' are tempered by benign nationalism.

It is all too probable that one of the endearing, perhaps enduring, clichés of the end of the twentieth century will be the postmodern/electronic age concept of image chaos: the progressively unshocking shocks of overloaded layers, bizarre juxtapositions and oppositions, forgeries and thefts, wrenches of time and location, and dislocations of function and meaning. There are tangible models everywhere: the streetsounds of a modern, Fourth World, *retronuevo* city like Miami; the recording studios of the Bombay film industry with its indiscriminate pile-ups of world music bites; the traverse of historical and religious divides and levels of technology in the music of Mali and Senegal.

'Flamenco in Sweden' is the way Alvin Toffler described it in *Future Shock* in 1970, the inevitable peculiarities that arise as a result of increasing geographical mobility. Music history has become, to a remarkable extent, a record and tape collection. Music is composed or performed with knowledge gleaned from recordings; records are made with fragments of music lifted from other records. Unnecessary, at the end of the twentieth century, to bring forty marines and a brass band; a single cassette, arriving in a new geographical location, can upturn musical traditions for good.

1 Eta Harich-Schneider, *A History of Japanese Music*, Oxford University Press, London, 1973

2 Emilie De Brigard, The History of Ethnographic Film, in *Principles of Visual Anthropology*, Mouton, Hague, 1975

3 Walter Benjamin, *Reflections*, Harcourt Brace Jovanovich, New York, 1978

4 Umberto Eco, *Faith In Fakes*, Secker & Warburg, London, 1986

5 Ramon Pelinski, 'Oriental Colouring In the Music of the Nineteenth Century', in *World Cultures and Modern Art*, Bruckmann, Munich, 1972

6 Alain Gheerbrant, *The Impossible Adventure*, Victor Gollancz, London, 1955

7 Klaus Wachsmann, 'Spencer to Hood: a changing view of non-European music', *Proceedings of the Royal Anthropological Institute of Great Britain and Ireland*, London, 1973

8 Opal Portfolios, London, 1986

9 Jon Hassell, sleeve notes to *Aka/Darbari/Java: Magic Realism*, Editions EG EGED 31, London, 1983

10 Karlheinz Stockhausen, 'World Music', In *The World of Music*, Vol. XXI. No. 1. Heinrichshofen's Verlag, Wilhelmshaven, 1979

11 Karl H. Worner, *Stockhausen: Life and Work*, Faber & Faber, London, 1973

12 Norman Lewis, *A Dragon Apparent*, Jonathan Cape, London, 1951

(Above) The Rolling Stones with African drummers, Hyde Park 1969

SELECTED DISCOGRAPHY

PARIS, AFRICA

Toure Kunda: *Natalia* (Celluloid)
Alpha Blondy: *Apartheid is Nazism* (Sterns)
Mory Kante: *Akwaba Beach* (Barclay)
Kassav: *Zouk is the Only Medicine We Have* (Greensleeves)
Pepe Kalle & Nyboma: *Moyibi* (Sterns)
Dede St Prix: *Mi Se Sa* (Mango)
Kanda Bongo Man: *Amour Fou* (Hannibal)
Manu Dibango: *Live: Happy Reunion* (Buda)
Ray Lema: *Nangadeef* (Mango)
Papa Wemba: *Papa Wemba* (Sterns Africa)

CUBA AND THE ROOTS OF SALSA

Johnny Pacheco: *Introducing Johnny Pacheco* (Caliente/Charly)
Tito Puente: *Un Poco Loco* (Concord Jazz Picante)
Various: *The Roots of Salsa* (Folklyric)
Irakere: *The Legendary Irakere In London – Live at Ronnie Scotts* (Jazz House)
Los Van Van: *Songo* (Mango)
Celia Cruz: *Introducing Celia Cruz* (Caliente)
Willie Colon: *Criollo* (RCA)
Oscar D'Leon: *Riquiti* (Dureco Benelux)
Ruben Blades: *Siembra* (Fania)
Joe Arroyo: *Rebellion* (World Circuit)

THE NEW COUNTRY SOUND

Steve Earle: *Copperhead Road* (MCA)
Randy Travis: *Storms Of Life* (WEA)
Lyle Lovett: *Pontiac* (MCA)
K. D. Lang: *Shadowland* (Sire)
Dwight Yoakam: *Buenos Noches From a Lonely Room* (Reprise)
Reba McEntire: *Reba* (MCA)
Nanci Griffith: *Lone Star State of Mind* (MCA)
Ricky Scaggs: *Personal Choice – I Love Country* (Epic)
Rosanne Cash: *Retrospective 1979–1989* (CBS)
Gram Parsons (featuring Emmylou Harris); *Grievous Angel* (Reprise)

ALGERIAN RAI

Cheba Fadela with Cheb Sahraoui: *You Are Mine* (Mango)
Cheb Khaled: *Hada Raykoum* (Triple Earth)
Cheb Mami: *Prince of Rai* (Triple Earth)
Chaba Zahouania: *Nights Without Sleeping* (Mango)
Various: *Rai Rebels* (Earthworks)
Cheb Kader: *Cheb Kader* (Blue Silver – Melodie)
Messaoud Bellemou: *Le Pere Du Rai* (World Circuit)

THE INTERNATIONAL TRADE IN NEW MUSIC

King Sunny Ade: *Synchro System* (Island)
Sipho Mabuse: *Sipho Mabuse* (Virgin)
Various: *Zimbabwe Frontline* (Earthworks)
Aster Aweke: *Aster* (Triple Earth)
Sam Mangwana: *Aladji* (Syllart)
Fela Kuti: *Everything Scatter* (Phonogram)
Various: *New Roots* (Stylus)
Nusrat Fateh Ali Khan: *Qawwal and Party Vol I and II* (Womad/Realworld); *Shahen-Shah* (Realworld)
Tabu Ley: *Rochereau* (Shanachie)
Ofra Haza: *Shaday* (WEA)

THE MUSIC OF WEST AFRICA

Youssou N'Dour: *Immigrés* (Earthworks); *The Lion* (Virgin)
Toumani Diabate: *Kaira* (Hannibal)
Ali Farka Toure: *Ali Farka Toure* (World Circuit)
Baaba Maal: *Djam Leeli* (Rogue)
Salif Keita *Soro* (Sterns Africa); *Ko-Yan* (Mango)
Les Ambassadeurs: *Mandjou* (Celluloid)
Etoile De Dakar: *Tolou Badou Ndiaye* (ET)
Various: *Mali Music* (Sterns Africa)
Kassy Made: *Fode* (Sterns Africa)
Baaba Maal and Dande Lenol: *Wango* (Syllart)

A LIVING TRADITION IN HUNGARY AND BULGARIA

Trio Bulgarka: *The Forest is Crying* (Hannibal)
Bulkana: *The Music of Bulgaria* (Hannibal)
Various: *Le Mystère De Voix Bulgares Vol I + II* (4 AD)
Marta Sebestyen: *Marta Sebestyen* (Hannibal)
Vujicsics: *Serbian Music from Southern Hungary* (Hannibal)
Various: *The Fifth Hungarian Dance House Festival* (Hungaroton)
Muzsikas: *Nem Arrol Hajnallik, Amerrol Hajnallot* (Hungaroton)

MUSIC AND POLITICS IN LATIN AMERICA

Ruben Blades: *Buscando America* (Elektra)
Mercedes Sosa: *Todaviva Cantamos!* (Tropical Music/Polygram)
Gabino Palomares: *El Cancionero Popular – Amparo Ochoa and the Folkloristas* (Discos Pueblo Mexico)
Milton Nascimento: *Corazon Americano* (Tropical Music/Polygram)
Atahualpa Yupanqui: *Basta Ya* (Le Chant du Monde)
Violeta Parra: *Las Ultimas Composiciones de Violeta Parra* (RCA Victor)
Silvio Rodriguez: *Dias Y Flores* (Hannibal)
Inti Illimani: *Inti Illimani 8. Cancion Para Matar Una Calebra* (Movieplay Spain)
Various: *April In Managua – The Central American Peace Concert* (Varagram Holland)
Silvio Rodriguez and Pablo Milanes: *Envivo in Argentina* (Polydor)

SOUTH AFRICA'S SHADOW CULTURE

Mahlathini and the Mahotella Queens: *Thokozile* (Earthworks)
Mahlathini: *The Lion of Soweto* (Earthworks)
Johnny Clegg: *Shadowman* (EMI)
Various: *The Indestructible Beat of Soweto Vol I + II* (Earthworks)
Soul Brothers: *Jive Explosion* (Earthworks)
Ladysmith Black Mambazo: *Induku Zethu* (Greensleeves)
Hugh Masekela: *Techno-Bush* (Jive Afrika)

Stimela: *Look Listen and Decide* (Celluloid)
Malombo: *Malombo* (Kijima)
Various: *South African Trade Union Worker Choirs* (Rounder)

BLUES FOR THE EIGHTIES

Jeff Healey Band: *See The Light* (Arista)
Robert Cray: *Strong Persuader/Don't Be Afraid of the Dark* (Mercury)
Albert Collins: *Ice Pickin'* (Sonet)
Albert Collins, Robert Cray, Johnny Copeland: *Showdown* (Sonet)
Buddy Guy: *Chess Masters* (Chess)
Stevie Ray Vaughan: *Live Alive* (Epic)
B. B. King: *The Best of B. B. King* (MCA)
John Lee Hooker: *The House of the Blues* (Chess)
Howlin' Wolf: *Chess Masters* (Chess)
Muddy Waters: *The Best of Muddy Waters* (Chess)